The l Adventurer and Her Inconvenience

A first-time cycle trip across Europe

Donna Marie Ashton

Dedication

For Iain, with all my love.

Contents

Acknowledgements

Biggest thanks go to Iain. You're not actually an inconvenience at all.

Thanks to the rest of my wonderful family. Your support both during the trip and the writing process has helped to make this book a reality.

To my editor, Sue Browning. Thank you for your guidance, diligence and attention to detail.

Thanks to all the people who helped with logistics, took care of things back home for us while we were away and followed our progress.

Thanks to Solo and Polo. If only we had been as reliable as you.

Thanks to the talented Dave Freeland of Toonerisms for creating the perfect illustrations to complement this book. Your patience has been legendary. www.toonerisms.com

Chapter 1
In the beginning

There I was, again, trying to jump off to stabilise the bike before it fell over. There I was, again, failing to prevent the inevitable. Once again, the full force of a heavily laden bike, carrying all of my belongings, crashed sideways to the ground. This happened every time the gradient was so steep that I eventually lost momentum. No matter how hard I stood on the pedal, I had neither the weight, power nor strength to make the wheels continue to go round. Carrying an extra 20kg or so on a bike ride all the way to the Black Sea was clearly not going to be easy. Just as well we had six months to get there, was a common early thought. Perhaps we should have prepared a bit better, was another.

As if our own inadequacies weren't enough, our progress that first cycling day was slowed down further by the wind. Sometimes from the side, sometimes head on, but never helpfully from the rear. Even a seasoned cyclist can be challenged by the wind. This combination of wind and inexperience was a nightmare, an accident waiting to happen. Our laden bikes, with panniers acting like giant sails, often got thrown to the side without our consent (a bit like how wind can affect a lorry more than a car, despite the lorry being heavier). On a frequent basis this sent us across the road and potentially into the path of oncoming traffic. Head-winds just make cycling harder. That day, when we stopped pedalling, our bikes rolled backwards. What an idiot thinking we could get there in just six months, crept into the thoughts. Definitely should have prepared much better, was another!

Late morning and having established that the youth hostel at Morlaix was a bit on the pricey side (and we couldn't really afford to keep pushing the boat out), we discovered that the nearest campsite was 64km away. Compared to wild camping, at least if we reached a proper campsite, our 64km reward would be a nice warm shower. With the pressure on, and our "start slow – build gradually – take it easy" plan already out of the window, we continued to tackle the hills and be buffeted by the wind of Brittany. Probably not the ideal scenario to encounter my first ever faux asthma attack. I seriously couldn't breathe out properly and every breath was accompanied by an audible whistle. I had no option but to get off the bike and adopt the half-lean, half-collapse position. This was followed immediately by my first ever panic attack at the realisation that Iain was already way ahead of me and nowhere to be seen (he had the phone). I was in no fit state to shout – he's deaf anyway – and I didn't have anything even remotely useful in our "comprehensive" first aid kit! After what seemed like an eternity of inadequate levels of oxygen, Iain eventually came back to find me, still doubled over, but nicely timed to when I felt "almost normal" again. I have no idea what that was about; it was incredibly scary. These certainly weren't the type of "new firsts" I was hoping for when setting out.

We were looking forward to getting to Morlaix, after which, Iain announced, the map showed the cycle route followed a canal, which would obviously be much flatter. We had terrible trouble locating the cycle route out of town. Eventually, after several loops involving the same scenery, we met a fellow cyclist called Xavier. Having lived in London for fourteen years, he spoke perfect English. He'd also lived and worked in Holland, so he recognised our Koga bikes. In fact, one of the bikes in his collection of seven was a previous model. Iain and Xavier chatted for the couple of uphill kilometres to the start of the route; I had serious trouble keeping up. Xavier's parting comment to us was that it was an honour to accompany us at the start of such an incredible adventure and challenge. What a nice guy. At least he seemed to have more faith in us than I did at that precise moment. With so many problems in just the first half of the first real day, I was not feeling anywhere near as certain.

There was no canal just outside Morlaix. It was a disused railway line, and it wasn't flat. It was miles and miles of uphill gravelly track. It really was relentless – admittedly not steep, but nonetheless definitely uphill, and with a load on, it was hard work.

Before we set off we had decided that we would each cycle at our own pace, and whoever was fastest/in the lead would periodically stop at suitable points or junctions to wait for the other. It would be no more fair for me to expect Iain to cycle at my snail's pace than for him to expect me to try to keep up with him. This worked well for us and we hope went some way to making the tour work for both of us without boredom (Iain) or injury (me).

Every time I caught up with Iain waiting patiently by the side of the track, he'd ask how I was as I approached. All I could manage was a stream, no, torrent, of swearing and moaning about the seemingly never-ending bloody hill, the weight of the bike, the never-ending hill, the crap gears, the never-ending hill, the cold weather, the never-ending hill, the wind, the never-ending hill, the idiotic map, the never-ending hill, my useless legs, the never-ending hill, my aching legs, the bloody stupid, crappy, flipping never-ending hill, which wasn't a flat bloody canal! (for reasons of good taste I have omitted the f-word which punctuated most, no, each and every, moan). Poor Iain! When he was sure I had recovered and was ready, we'd set off again and the cycle of cycling (excuse the pun) swearing and stopping continued again, for hours.

Then, at the point where I really believed my flabby legs were actually made of jelly, had absolutely zero energy left and really was struggling (I had even stopped swearing!), we suddenly, like a wonderful unexpected gift, broached the top of the hill and saw we were in for some well-earned downhill sections. Hurrah! We cheered, laughed and felt instantly uplifted. Neither of us felt we could go any further uphill even if we tried.

Iain (with much more bike experience than me) went a lot faster downhill than I dared, but after a few hundred metres I became more confident and started to gain speed. Think pride before a fall! And fall I did. It all happened so fast – one minute I was upright, the next minute the bike was listing sideways at a 45-degree angle, and there was no way with that weight that I could do anything to counteract gravity. I found myself luckily not seriously injured, but with my right leg trapped under the bike and blood seeping through my trouser knee. Shaken, I managed to wiggle out from under the heavy frame and check myself out. A lucky escape, I decided, but chose not to look at the knee in too much detail until later. I'm sure the panniers saved me from further injury and cushioned the fall of the bike. Luckily, it was undamaged and so I decided to walk along pushing it for a bit – at least until I stopped shaking. Once I was feeling a bit more normal, I had no option really but to get back on and pedal. After all, Iain was probably at the campsite by now!

It was a bit unpleasant. With every pedal turn my trousers kept sticking, unsticking and re-sticking to my knee. Maybe I should have had a look at it and put on a plaster after all. Believe it or not, even though we both used to work on the emergency ambulances in a former life, and I'm more than happy dealing with other people's injuries, blood, gore and misfortunes, I'm not so good with my own (or, come to think of it, any form of vomit, no matter who it belongs to!). I was now much more wary of going faster again. It would be absolutely fair to say that I was, at this stage, totally incompetent at anything resembling good bike handling. We hadn't even covered 50km; what on earth made me think I would be capable of 5,000km?

At the bottom of the hill, at a road junction, Iain was talking to a cycle tourist who was travelling in the other direction. Having established from him that the campsite we were heading to was closed, we had no option but to head to another, no further in distance but off-route and (you've guessed it) up another (even steeper this time) bloody hill. Swearing recommenced.

The thought of a nice warm shower coupled with the fact that we were actually nearly there was what kept us going. I had to resort to getting off the bike and pushing as it was so steep. On the positive side, at least pushing the bike was using different muscles. Iain managed to cycle the whole way but in the process injured his knee. As we rolled together down the driveway of the campsite celebrating our first 64km, we were met by huge *"FERMÉ"*, aka "CLOSED" signs. *Merde, merde* and more bloody, f***ing, *merde!*

On the bright side, at least we could say we survived our first ever day of cycle touring. To say it was without injury or incident would be seriously pushing the boundaries of truth. To say it had been pleasant for either of us would be an outright lie. Just what had we got ourselves into!?

Chapter 2
Planning

Sadly, our nest was well and truly empty. Not only had the kids selfishly left home a year or so ago, but our faithful Labrador had gone and unexpectedly kicked the bucket. I'm not denying, we both had a huge crevice of a void to fill. Having been married for 25 years, most people would probably celebrate their anniversary with a meal or a party. We now felt the time was right to celebrate our marriage by doing something out of the ordinary, something for ourselves. We wanted to do something we had never done before and it had to include travel. We also both felt the need to challenge ourselves, take ourselves out of our comfort zone, partly to fill a void, but maybe also to prove that we weren't really that old, after all. Surely first-time adventures didn't have to just be the domain of the twenty-somethings or experienced, gnarly, bearded men? We had missed out on the gap-year phenomenon first time round. We were not going to miss out on the opportunity of something out of the ordinary now.

All sorts of ideas were flung between the two of us. Most were quickly discarded due to cost and the limited time we thought we had to do it in (I say thought because we hadn't yet arranged work cover). Car and other vehicles were ruled out as being no real physical challenge and far too expensive. Trekking was ruled out as being too slow, and backpacking, just so ordinary! Bikes seemed like the perfect mode of transport for what we wanted to achieve. Now all we needed was a destination. Europe seemed the obvious choice – no visas, no flights, some familiarity. Thinking it would be a good idea, I printed off two maps of Europe and issued each of us with a highlighter pen and we each set about marking out our dream route and destinations. I was hoping our route would then be obvious. Unfortunately, they were completely different! Funnily enough, we did both want to go to Italy, though we didn't actually go there in the end.

After much debate and searching for a route we could both agree on, we found that there existed a wonderful network of European cycle routes which criss-crossed their ways across most of the continent. We chose EuroVelo 6 as it was described on the EuroVelo website as *"from the Atlantic to the Black Sea, [EV6] is one of our most popular routes and it's little wonder why: coasts, rivers, castles and a nice flat topography make it every cycle tourists' dream journey"*. It runs along various major European rivers (the Loire, the Rhine, the Danube) right across the entire continent of Europe and sounded perfect. I particularly liked the nice flat topography part. So, despite the fact that neither Iain nor myself had ever been further than a few miles on a bike before, we decided that our first ever cycle tour destination would be the Black Sea. This meant a journey through ten different European countries and a distance of about 5,000km. We were so excited and couldn't wait to get going.

We decided that such an attempt would be a good opportunity to raise both awareness and a bit of sponsor money for a local charity. After a thorough investigation and much mulling, we outlined our plans to CHICKS – a charity offering respite holidays to children with serious life-quality challenges (such as bereavement or being a carer for a parent). We were particularly impressed with the continuation of contact the charity offers the children at other times of year, such as birthday cards and Christmas presents, and the way it continues to support them for many years. The fact I didn't even own a bike (other than the kids' old one I inherited from my daughter) seemed immaterial. Failure was now not an option.

Having not done this type of thing before, we had a lot to learn, and a great many decisions to make. Other cycle tourists (we later found out these were known as credit card tourers) carry minimal clothing, stay in hotels and eat out. They also tend to be Lycra-clad racing-bike enthusiasts, with super-light bikes, where speed and destination is their main priority; often they don't even stop to pee! Our daily budget (or lack of it) meant our options were pretty much reduced to carrying all of our own equipment and camping, a completely different type of bike tour. Secretly, our dislike of the Lycra look and preference to use a toilet may also have influenced our decision! We were looking forward to the journey itself and hoped to have time to experience the different places along the way. Our loads would need to be as light as possible, so everything we took with us would need to be essential to earn its way into the panniers. However, we didn't want to compromise on comfort. We were going to be away for six months and felt a decent bed and chair would actually be important. And so, here began our winter of ridiculous obsession with how much everything weighed versus did we really need it? We were to leave on the 3rd of April 2015; we had just four months to get organised.

It seemed sensible to sort out some bikes first. I'm only small (and that's probably an over-estimation), so my first visit to the bike shop was a bit disappointing as they didn't have anything which properly fitted me. However, I've kind of got used to this. As a child, every bike I was ever gifted for my (end of August) birthday was always supplied as being "the right size to grow into "("perfect for next year's holiday"). Any bikes of mine in adulthood were always my own kids' outgrown cast-offs. So, rather than being miffed about the lack of suitable-sized bikes, I managed my oversized bike trial with ease around the city and hills of Exeter and was really impressed by the fact it actually had gears which worked (new one on me), and I marvelled at how much easier hills become if you have them.

To cut a long story short, by the time we had mismatched and changed parts of one bike for another (in order to fit me), the cost would have added up into the bracket of more expensive specialist touring bikes. So we decided to treat ourselves and order specialist touring bikes from Holland. At least I should get one that didn't need altering and that really fitted me. After many measurements of leg, height, arm reach (all new phenomena to us novice cyclists), our order was sent and we waited, like excited children waiting for Christmas, for what seemed like an eternity but was actually just a few weeks. When we arrived at the shop to collect them, the staff were even more like kids (apparently they hadn't seen our particular bike in the flesh, only in catalogues) and they were more impressed by the overall quality (and were especially bike geeky about a few of the special technical designs) than they expected to be. Unfortunately, I didn't really have the same enthusiasm towards my own brand shiny new bike. All the time Iain and the staff were raving about how amazing they were, I couldn't help but be thinking – isn't it just, well, a bit too big! Not wishing to let on just how amateur I was to all this cycle malarkey, I just thought, well, I'm used to big bikes, and I'm sure they know what they are doing (being bike specialists and/or from Holland and all), and at least it is a girl's frame, so I can actually get on and off it without causing myself a mischief. And so I kept my thoughts to myself.

Having bought the bikes, we thought about doing a bit of extra fitness training. After all, we were planning to be on them for about 5,000km. Seeing as we live on Dartmoor, combined with the fact it was winter, we quickly decided it might not be a very pleasant option, but we thought a few short rides out on good-weather days to test how the bikes performed might be a good plan. Earlier the previous year, at great expense, Dartmoor National Park had launched a series of marked (family-friendly) cycleways around the edge of Dartmoor, so we thought they would be a good testing ground. We took the one which allegedly skirts around the edge of the Haytor area, to avoid the more strenuous hills and have a pleasant afternoon on little-used lanes. If the signposts had actually pointed towards a road instead of between two roads then we might not have ended up down in Ashburton on a dual carriageway with an almighty six-mile uphill section for our first little jaunt out. Still, at least we found out how the bikes behaved and the gears certainly earned their keep. We also discovered for sure that even though we could not physically get any more red in the face, we didn't actually burst any blood vessels, or worse. Note to self at this point was "don't rely on signposts", and I think we were slightly reassured that although it was a hill we hadn't been expecting that day, we did manage it. Any plans for further winter Dartmoor bike fitness training were immediately shelved. Instead we planned to start the real tour with a low mileage and build up as we got fitter. Which, as you already know, didn't happen!

Our panniers were ordered and arrived. There's much discussion out there amongst cycle tourists about which are the best. As novices we made our decision: we needed something waterproof and hopefully with at least a few compartments so we could organise our stuff a bit. For those that are interested in what equipment we took, (maybe planning or dreaming of your own first tour or comparing what you may have already used), I have provided our kit list as an appendix. Likewise, those of you who are not interested can feel safe in the knowledge that you can conveniently ignore it guilt-free and not be bogged down by techie bike or camping talk at the end of a good old-fashioned tale.

We spent many hours testing tents at outdoor camping shops, much more fun than combatting the Christmas shopping crowds. Although I am small, Iain is tall, so we went for the luxury of a tent with a three-man sleeping compartment and an extra porch area to house all of our panniers overnight and to cook in should the weather be inclined to be a bit British. The first tent arrived and was so big it could have housed an elephant, so we returned it. I know I said we wanted a bit of comfort as we were due to be away for so long, but that was probably taking it too far, and (like I said) we had become a little bit obsessive about weighing everything. We could (as Iain's teachers used to say) do better and find something lighter.

Our attention turned to clothing and working out the minimum items to be both practical and lightweight. It helped that most of our tour was planned for the summer months: a couple of fleeces, a feather jacket, a hat, some gloves and a waterproof jacket and trousers were our only cold/wet-weather items. With both of us having an aversion to being constrained within sleeping bags, we decided (based on reading about another touring couple's experience) that a feather duvet would suit our requirements and could be easily squashed into a really small space. Sleeping mats (the thickest we could carry) were received and I set about crafting a nifty sheet-type envelope (out of an old duvet cover) which would hold our mats together and stop them sliding around the tent floor.

We decided against using GPS and went instead for the old-fashioned maps. There were two reasons for this: one was we were not sure how much electricity we would have access to (so continuously charging phones or tablets might not be an option), and two because we like maps – they can't really go wrong, can they? They were specialist bike maps which showed the route plus a few miles either side, and they fitted neatly onto the see-through map pocket on Iain's handlebar bag. I opted, rather craftily, to have a handlebar bag with no map pocket, not because I can't map-read (before you assume that) but because I am the one who for the last twenty-five years has always been the map-reader on our various car jaunts across Europe and I fancied a change. Plus (and this may be the real reason) it was a nice small bag, which when off the bike looked more like an almost normal handbag and less like a crate to be lugging around when sightseeing in cities or out for an evening meal. I'm sure by now you've worked out that we really didn't want to look like geeky cyclists all of the time.

So, with our kit (clothing, bedding, tent, chairs, cooking equipment, maps, wash-kits, first aid/medication kits, washing-up liquid, washing line, camera, phone and the rest of it) all assembled, we then had to see if there was any likelihood whatsoever that it would actually fit in the panniers and if we could collectively carry it, let alone manage it all on a bike.

It turned out that it did, and we could. Well, eventually we could.

Chapter 3
And they're nearly off

It was surprising to some that we didn't wish to start our epic trip from home and cycle along the delightful A38 dual carriageway to catch our ferry at Plymouth. Instead, our daughter and fiancée kindly gave us a lift in a hire van. On a very wet and gloomy April morning, whilst lifting the bikes into the van, they both commented that my bike looked, well, a bit big for me. Too late to change it now, I mustered, "I've been out on it, it's fine." "It's fine," echoed Iain.

It certainly felt different boarding a ferry on a bike compared to driving on; it actually felt like the beginning of a real adventure, predominantly because you are not allowed to ride on and have to push all 35kg/42kg (mine/Iain's) of it up the ramp! (5st 7lbs / 6st 8lbs in old money and this does include the actual bike). We were directed to a section at the side (never before noticed) with a metal railing and pieces of varying-quality rope for you to secure your bike with for the journey. With that all in order, we made our way up the metal staircases to the outside decks so we could wave to our daughter. I think it was only at that moment that we both realised the gravity and length of the task that we had set ourselves, mainly due to the confirmation of the time we would be spending away from our daughter. So, although we were both excited to be beginning our trip at last, as the boat began to pull away, we were both in floods of soppy-date tears.

The stunningly substandard ferry breakfast brought us back down to earth. Luckily, we were soon going to be eating like kings with all the goodies that France had to offer. We were going to be on bikes and could (more or less) eat whatever we liked. Iain joked at wanting to be the first touring cyclist to put on weight during a tour. I was mainly just looking forward to visiting many *boulangeries* (I like cake). Actually, we both just like food – not really into quantity but definitely into quality, which is probably why Italy was on both of our cycle tour wish lists – well, for now, we would just have to make do with France, as we were not going to Italy.

I naively thought pushing two-thirds of my own body weight down a ramp and off the ferry would be easier than pushing it on. I was proven wrong, with aching hands from tightly gripping the brake handles in order to prevent a fully laden bike careering out of control and ploughing into the back of a line of cars. At least, I thought, most of the way we should be pedalling and not pushing. Surely that will be easier.

And so, ramp successfully negotiated, we mounted our bikes on the French tarmac and were waved in front of the cars to join the customs queue behind the other cyclists, a couple of young lads and another couple. As seems normal for fellow cycle tourists, we all asked each other where we heading and eyeballed each other's luggage and bikes. The couple gave us a tenner towards our charity and the lads looked thoroughly impressed (read disbelief) that our destination was further than theirs! Now it felt like we had really started. With passports checked, all the bike riders were individually smiled at and waved through. All except Iain, that is. The head behind the counter told him to wait, then the rest of her (including head) came out of her cabin (to have a better look at him) and decided he was to be escorted to the Maritime Police building across the road. No, I was not allowed to accompany him. Yes, I was allowed to wait outside the building with the bikes. Perhaps we hadn't really got started yet, after all.

For over half an hour my mind was wandering and pondering many different, mostly not good, mistaken identity, end-of-trip before it's even started scenarios whilst simultaneously trying to restrain the bikes (with their bags acting as huge sails) from being blown over by a strong buffeting wind. Iain then appeared, looking serious, with two Maritime Police Officers and told me he had to report to the *gendarmes* in town and wait (most probably in a cell), until a lawyer arrived for him. The two officers grinned (crikey, they're enjoying our misfortune, I thought) and then Iain came clean, saying it was only a joke. Apparently his official questioning was only a few minutes long, but the officers were bike fanatics and the rest of the time they were just in awe of the distance we intended to cover, so most subsequent questions had been on the detail of our route, and they now wanted to have a look at our bikes. He was only stopped in the first place as part of a random anti-terrorism initiative. Phew!

The hill out of the ferry port of Roscoff was a bit of a wake-up call, our first real fully laden experience. Iain took the lead (after all, he had the maps), and succeeded in making me chuckle and kept me amused by selecting a gear where his legs were going around more than three times for each of my one! It looked really funny, but as a consequence, he was cycling slower than I wanted to go, but I had neither the extra oomph nor the space (due to overtaking cars) required to overtake him, which meant I kept nearly crashing into his back wheel. I have no idea how I managed to avoid crashing into him or didn't end up walking. At this rate, it could turn out to be an eventful trip.

The weather was absolutely horrendous, blowing a hooley, with sideways rain lashing and stinging any tiny bits of exposed flesh. Just getting into town was a challenge, so I think we were both secretly pleased when we discovered that there were no campsites open in early April in Roscoff. Seeing as it was late afternoon anyway, it was the perfect excuse for a night in a hotel. Our bikes spent their first night out in the elements locked up in a little courtyard. We spent the first evening unpacking and repacking and checking our bags. I'm not really sure why, but it seemed like a sensible thing to be doing. Then we went out for dinner to celebrate getting started. Well, almost started!

Fully satiated after a wonderful hotel breakfast (total antithesis of the ferry experience), we were keen to get going. The weather, thankfully, had eased off, and although a bit gusty occasionally, it was at least now dry. We made ourselves grin by giving the bikes the quintessential French look by attaching baguettes to our luggage racks. One more stop at the grocer's, who were in the middle of painting the ceiling, with full-on stepladders and a big bucket of paint to dodge, during opening hours, and we were actually, finally, really off, with lunch and dinner safely stashed away in my pannier bags.

We were considering the first part of our route, south through Brittany towards Nantes, as being our training section, our aim being to stick to a reasonable and easily achievable daily amount of kilometres (all of the route markers were in km and it seemed sensible not to have the complication of converting everything from miles) and then to gradually increase it as we became fitter and more used to the rigours of cycle touring. If only it had panned out that way. Then we wouldn't have found our knackered selves, late on the evening of day one, arriving at a closed campsite at the top of a hill.

Chapter 4
The first night

Meanwhile, with no campsite marked on the map for at least another 50km, there was absolutely NO way either of us would make it. We were now in the middle of nowhere: no other houses, shops, hotels or anything remotely brick-like. We would just have to wild camp near here and go without our much-looked-forward-to shower. (Damn it! We could have done that at the bottom of the hill!)

When the huge bearded owner (read Giant Haystacks) suddenly appeared out of the woods and invited us to pitch up and said he would put the hot water on, we both could have hugged him (it was probably the food bits in the beard that put us off!). Iain bought a couple of cans of cassoulet for breakfast from the unopened shop. And we pitched our tent for the first night and headed off for our keenly anticipated shower.

Campsite showers, in my opinion, should have at least one hook (to hang your belongings on), and preferably they should have a screen or curtain or something behind which they should place the hook (in order to keep the hooked-up belongings dry). They should be clean, without other people's pubic hair, not have blocked (with matted hair) plugholes and, in an ideal world, should have a shelf or somewhere inside the shower part to place your shampoo/soap etc. A door or additional curtain for privacy is quite a nice touch too. It is also preferable that if they insist on putting in timed push buttons that the time limit given is longer than five seconds between presses and you get to choose the temperature of your shower, rather than one (usually cold) temperature fits all.

Thankfully, this hastily opened just for us shower came up trumps and had all of the above features, except the choice of temperature. Rather surprisingly, it was just too hot! And with no way to alter it, we both had to gradually get our arms used to being burnt before we could kind of throw water over the rest of our bodies with our hands, before eventually plucking up the courage to get our hair wet and washed and our scalps and the rest of us scalded! We came out much cleaner and feeling much warmer, which was a good thing, but looking decidedly lobsteresque.

On a long-distance trip like ours we could only carry a small amount of clothing. This meant that we each only had three T-shirts with us, and of course, cycling all day does result in a sweaty Betty. So, part of our routine (most easily and quickly done in the shower with shampoo) was to hand-wash the T-shirt and cycle shorts from that day and leave them outside to dry overnight. We bunged all of our clothes in a washing machine too from time to time (when stopping on a campsite for more than one night).

So, laundry duties attended to, and towels and washing hung over our bikes, we set about preparing and eating our first evening meal and then collapsing into a heap in bed at about 9pm, looking forward to the bliss of a rest.

Now you would think that if you are absolutely, completely and utterly exhausted you wouldn't have any trouble whatsoever sleeping. Not so! Iain's knee, previously injured on the last hill, and his hip were so incredibly painful that he was almost in tears. (I knew it was bad, he is most definitely NOT a whinger.) Paracetamol and ibuprofen did not seem to make even the slightest bit of difference. We rigged up "clothing" pillows, in the absence of real ones, to cushion it. He actually said, "I think it's over. I don't know what I've done, but it's not good." At which point I genuinely felt it was the end of the trip (Iain's definitely NOT a quitter either) and we were both absolutely gutted. It was over before it had even properly begun.

I was reminded of one previous adventure-type tour I had attempted which had ended in a first-day failure too. When our kids were about 11 (Aaron) and 9 (Mairead), Iain had to go away for work so the kids and I planned to walk the 177-mile Offa's Dyke path from north to south Wales. Our Labrador, Ember, and her young puppy, Woody, would accompany us too. Aaron welded together a trolley in which the puppy could sleep when tired and which could also carry the dog food (which is quite a lot for two weeks) and the tent. So we felt well prepared. We would each carry a backpack with our own clothes, food and sleeping bags. All ready and excited, we set off, only to find that for the entire first day, the footpath was narrower than the trolley (it was such a lovely wide path on the web picture!), so Aaron and I had to carry the blinking trolley all day. We didn't get as far as the proper campsite for the first night and ended up pitched in the corner of a cattery's front garden. Ember then had some type of allergic reaction and her face swelled, making her look more like a hippopotamus than a Labrador. Worryingly, she was also unable to breathe, so we had to call out a vet pronto for some serious antihistamines. Just to cheer us up, the cattery owner informed us that the footpath didn't widen for at least another ten miles. Unable to carry two dogs, dog food, tent and a trolley, we all decided to call it a day. It seemed now as if history was repeating itself. Perhaps I was only cut out for one-day adventures.

As the night in our first French campsite wore on, it began to feel pretty cold. We put on more and more layers of clothes, and by dawn I was wearing the merino wool long-sleeve top and merino wool leggings that I started with, plus a fleece hat, fleece gloves, two fleeces (one of which I had managed to expertly manoeuvre a foot and calf into each armhole without lifting up the duvet, thus preventing any cold air from getting in), a down feather jacket, my only two pairs of socks and a pair of trousers.

Iain disturbed most of my first night's sleep. Firstly, he was snoring, really loudly (normal behaviour for him), but I had stupidly left my earplugs in the outer tent and it was just too cold to get them – so my own fault. Then he started groaning due to his knee, then groaning due to the cold, then shivering (and to think earlier I said he wasn't a whinger!), and for some annoying reason, he kept insisting on moving off his bigger sleeping mat and onto my smaller one, forcing me onto the cold floor at the side of the tent. In addition to all of the Iain-related sleep barriers, when not going for comedy value, the other reason I couldn't sleep was because every time I tried to straighten my legs, my thighs hurt, a lot.

As we ventured out of the tent not long after dawn, as we couldn't stand being awake in the tent for a minute longer, and in the greatest need of a very warm drink, we saw our T-shirts and towels frozen rigidly solid. No wonder we were blinking cold!

We heated up the tins of cassoulet, which Iain loved for some reason and I thought resembled baked beans with a variety of pet foods to try in it. It was, in its defence, at least hot and filling and was quick and easy to prepare, which with frozen fingers (and not the fishy variety) was a godsend. Then we began packing everything up in order to set off again. It took us almost forever to get organised and ready. It certainly took longer to pack up and get everything back in its place in those panniers than to pull it out and get set up.

After a quick acupuncture session on Iain's knee (I'm an acupuncturist, in case you were wondering how we found one on an unopened campsite in the middle of the French countryside), a plaster on mine, which wasn't serious but I didn't like the way it kept sticking to my trousers, and with both of us taking a bucket load of painkillers (neither of us usually takes anything if we can help it!), we felt a million dollars and ready to hit the road. I lie. Actually, we felt physically like we could hobble on, as long as we didn't overdo it again and we got to stop for a morning coffee, croissant and, later on, a decent lunch. Mentally we were up for it, as long as we got to stop for a morning coffee, croissant and, later on, a decent lunch. And so, despite it having looked like it was all over the previous night, off we set again in search of a café.

Chapter 5
Naming

And so, we set off in slight pain but in surprisingly good spirits, anticipating a much easier day, dreaming of a delightful French café or two and the long-awaited flat canal section. Within a few kilometres, in the village of Poullaouen, we were sitting outside, warming ourselves in glorious sunshine, with coffee and croissants, followed by more coffee/hot chocolate and croissants and the opportunity to write our diaries. Compared to yesterday, this was bliss and, well, just more civilised. Now I could see we might make it after all. Well, that's how it was until we tried to stand up. My legs just refused to straighten, preferring a halfway-onto-the-toilet pose for comfort. Iain's knee was clearly excruciatingly painful as he had to suddenly grab the table midway up. Whereas normally I would have to encourage, almost beg, him to take pain-relief pills, he was immediately asking where they were and taking them despite it being three hours too early to do so!

Tentatively, we got back on the saddle and slowly started pedalling. Progress was going to be slow. Luckily we had six months and it was never our intention to be breaking any speed records or have any dreams of appearing in the famous Guinness Book. Once back on the old railway line, I'd like to say things improved, or that we settled into it, or we felt any sense of achievement. We didn't. It was horrible. Iain was in pain, I was aching, we couldn't go faster than a snail's pace and, just to cheer us up further, we were now also contending with more uphill and a head-wind so cold it was causing me to get an ice-cream-freeze head. And so the swearing recommenced, nicely punctuated by whingeing, and now also crying (such attractive traits!). This was such a low point, and so early on, too. It would appear that despite thinking I could achieve almost anything I set my mind to, I was not cut out for this type of thing, and the only thing I had in common with real adventurers was Ellen MacArthur's ability to blub when the going got tough. On the other hand, maybe I *was* cut out for this; I never once let Iain know I had been in tears. If this adventure was cut short I was determined it wasn't going to be my fault (what a weirdo!).

Completely knackered, at 4pm we rolled into a town called Carhaix-Plouguer, having covered the grand total of 17km. What a total embarrassment. We tried to justify this to ourselves by adding it to the previous day's mileage and averaging it as being more than we had expected to achieve on our first two days. With no campsite, the next one too far for us to get to at our current snail's pace, and, as reliably informed by the pharmacy signs, the temperature was already down into low single figures, we opted for a cheap hotel. There was no one on duty at the only hotel in town, just a handwritten note saying phone or come back after 7pm. The town was odd; nothing was open, not even a bar or café. Our only option was to cycle to the out-of-town industrial estate, where we were reliably informed, by the only person we could find, that there was a well-known American fast-food outlet, and kill three hours there. Not quite the culinary experience we were hoping for, but seeing as we hadn't eaten since our mid-morning croissants, we needed something. And with no confirmation that the hotel would have an available room, there was also the possibility we might have to spend the whole night there.

It was a long wait, and despite eating a couple of the larger burgers each, with large fries and ice cream, several coffee refills and having use of free wi-fi, and a long warm-up of the hands under the hand dryers, three hours was still a long wait. But at least we were out of the wind. Come 7pm, we were extremely relieved to discover the hotel had a room available. We were less relieved to find that the town was having some type of holiday the following day and that none of the shops (not even the *boulangerie*) would be open. The receptionist said that if there was any bread left over after breakfast, we could buy it from them. We were concerned about the word "if", and at breakfast managed to both eat our fill (read went overboard) and simultaneously secretly fill our small cool bag for lunch supplies. Funnily enough, there wasn't a whole loaf left for her to sell us after breakfast, so (out of guilt) we gratefully bought the half loaf which was left. "My goodness," she exclaimed in French, "your bike is the same size as your husband's and yet you are so small. I wish you good luck with your big bike!"

After a decent, ear-plugged, 9pm to 8am night's sleep, I was feeling much better. And after another acupuncture treatment and a warm soft bed with real pillows, Iain and his knee did too. His internet research the day before had suggested that, in case of knee pain, he could try raising his saddle, which he also did before setting off. Perhaps today we would get into it a bit more, finally get to that nice flat canal and make some progress?

Once out of town, the cycle route took us along some small country lanes. Initially we followed route markers, though, oddly, the distances on them didn't really seem to tally with our map, and then they vanished so we were left to our own devices. After several consultations with said map at a variety of junctions, we were sure we were heading in the right direction. Perhaps if our trust in signposts hadn't been destroyed by Dartmoor National Park's attempt at it, alarm bells might have rung and we would have correctly surmised that the lack of route markers was in fact a sign that we had wandered off route rather than dismissing it as being unimportant. And so it was that after several miles of pleasant country lanes, we ended up on a very long, muddy, narrow downhill section with hairpin bends (with built-up edges like a BMX track). Mmm, probably not the official route, we thought, just prior to being literally flung out onto the canal towpath. We had made it, but goodness only knows how or exactly where on the canal we were.

Prior to my tour research, I had no idea that long-distance cyclists go commando under their cycle shorts. Apparently, wearing pants or knickers will cause chafing. So we each bought ourselves a couple of pairs of fancy high-quality gel-panelled cycle shorts to wear under our "trying to look normal" shorts. I can confirm that we successfully avoided chafing. Although extremely grateful for the extra padding and slightly increased comfort the gel-panelled shorts gave me in the derrière department (compared with none), the legs on the shorts were excessively tight and were more than just uncomfortable. I appreciated that they needed to be tight, to prevent ride-up, but these seemed ridiculous. Perhaps I had just chosen a size too small? In a fit of frustration with them and the pain in my thighs, I took my Opinel knife and made four jagged cuts in each leg elastic. The thigh pain that had bugged me continuously for two and a half days disappeared in an instant.

With thighs and knees no longer an issue, we were able to appreciate the beautiful bright spring morning. Everything was greening up, and I could smell the sap rising in the beech trees which lined the canal. There was an abundance of primroses and other spring flowers. The birdlife was evident in song, from the recognisable cheerful chirping of the first swallows and hammering of the woodpeckers to the more unusual, unrecognisable to me, water-bird sounds. We saw guillemots diving, a snow-white stork-type bird and both a kestrel and several buzzards. We passed countless lock-keeper's cottages, some charming and immaculately kept, some still locked up for winter, and some in total disrepair. Now this was more like what we were expecting and we covered a few happy miles.

The previously lovely canal towpath then petered out and was replaced by a narrow muddy track, more suited to walking than cycling. I found it a challenge handling the bike in the sticky, clay-like soil, and several times thought I was going to fall off again. Worryingly, this time, if I did fall, there was a canal to fall into. Gradually, both the state of the path and the canal deteriorated, and on several occasions we had to lift our bikes over small fallen trees. It really was a dark and not very attractive section of neglected grimy, almost empty canal. Progress was, once again, slowed down, but at least I did manage to stay upright.

Then, without warning, as the path widened into a field, we found ourselves surrounded by hundreds of people. It turned out that the derelict Abbaye de Bon-Repos on the banks of the canal was used for historical re-enactments and was bustling with tourists. The pub and café were heaving, picnics were taking place on every available patch of grass, many people were arriving on foot from a multitude of different directions, and traffic chaos was ensuing over the only access road, which was a single-lane stone hump-back bridge. We stopped to take it all in for few minutes as it was a welcome antidote to the gloom of the previous section, and it gave us the opportunity to buy an amazing massive fresh brioche from a street stall.

On we pressed along more muddy track, followed by a hairpin-bend hill which went up and up and up. I had to resort to pushing. Iain stayed on the bike and reached the top first – people near the top were clapping him. I guessed the seat adjustment had worked.

Earlier, Iain had challenged me to name my bike by the end of the day. After all, he had a name for his. I'm actually giving the credit for the naming of Iain's bike to our son (Aaron) and his girlfriend (Abbie). They live in the south of France, and on a recent visit to them, without me, the three of them went for a few cycle rides in the mountains just north of Nice, their local village and Nice Plage. Apparently, Iain had cycled off ahead on his own for most of every trip and so they nicknamed him Solo. He decided that was a much more fitting name for a bike than a human, and so his new bike was named.

I wanted a name for mine that sounded right with Solo. After all, they were a double act. Equally, I was searching for something which also managed to represent her own individuality. If you're wondering, I wouldn't normally dedicate valuable brain time to such a mundane ridiculous activity or attach human emotional traits or gender to an inanimate object. But seeing as I was going to be actually relying on this bike for six months, and she was going to carry all of my luggage a bit like a pack-horse, it seemed to make sense to give her a pony kind of name, and so she was christened Polo.

We had a bit of trouble finding our campsite for the night but eventually did with the help of another cycle tourist on his way from Portugal to Paris. Timmy from the UK told us how he had set off in March and cycled through snow, and that this was the first day in two months when he wasn't cycling into a head-wind and he kind of missed it! No disrespect intended, Timmy, but we believed every word of it, just from looking at you. All three of us listened to a lovely French lady giving us very detailed directions and instructions in French (obviously), all nodding and agreeing and thanking her. And then, once she had left, we all realised we hadn't quite understood every bit of what she had said. Still, between us we managed to cobble together a rough idea, and luckily it worked out.

The campsite, although open, had no facilities except toilets. Our dinner options looked pretty bleak as there were no shops anywhere nearby either. It looked like we would be digging back into our remaining paltry breakfast rations topped up by the giant brioche we had bought back at the chateau. We pitched our tent and headed out on our unladen bikes down the lane, just in case we found a hidden bar, café or hotel. Nothing. But on the edge of the partially empty, very unattractive reservoir, we saw signs to a music festival, with a Buvette. Brilliant. We followed the signs, only to find two ladies packing away the last bits and pieces, a deserted set of instruments and a couple of tables filled with (what looked like) the off-duty rock musicians. Realising we had missed the event, we asked the two ladies if there was any chance of any left-over food and explained our predicament. We were told to sit down and were given a huge chunk of wonderful paté, exquisite nut bread, cheese bread and salad and told we could also buy a bottle of red wine for under 10 euros too, if we were thirsty. We were. What stars these ladies were. They had already packed up and they were more than happy to unpack this food just for us. After eating, the musicians (we were right) couldn't resist a little bit of strumming and jamming in front of their new (albeit tiny) audience before packing away too. What could have been a miserable evening turned out great after all.

And so followed another freezing cold night, wearing our full complement of clothing. With no showers on this campsite, a warm wash, a hot chocolate (me), hot coffee (Iain) and an enormous chunk of brioche was all we had to warm us up and get us going. Again, this took ages. Either we were going to have to get up earlier, my least favourite idea, or learn to pack up quicker, otherwise we would never make it to the Black Sea in time.

Chapter 6
Inconveniences

Our main issue on this third day was a general lack of sustenance, not something we had envisaged we would have to contend with in the country many consider as the culinary capital of the world. Since leaving the ferry we had not come across any open supermarkets and this was where we were hoping to stock up on things like porridge, pasta, rice and a cereal bar or six (note to self, next time set off with these items). Our plan was always to be carrying at least the basics and to top up our fresh produce on a daily basis. This would ensure, we thought, that we would get the best of both worlds, in terms of taste with local fresh produce, and be guaranteed to at least have a filling bowl of pasta (evening) or porridge (morning) to keep our energy reserves up, even if we didn't come across a bountiful farmers' market. So far, we had come across neither. We were burning calories but not adequately replacing them, we were cold, hungry and beginning to feel the strain from a lack of adequate sleep.

About two hours into riding on the third day my legs started shaking. Then all of my muscles shook, I had no strength and I was pretty sure I was close to vomiting. The only thing in my bag to eat was a teeny-tiny individual honey portion (I think it was left over from the ferry breakfast). After doing an impression of a demented bee and ensuring my tongue had probed out and consumed every last drop, I soon felt a little better but, as I'm sure you can imagine, the effects wore off again just as rapidly. We desperately needed to get more organised with our food supplies. Before setting off we had decided we would not resort, like many other successful cycle tourers (or other endurance adventurers), famous and otherwise, to surviving on just bread and jam, as they seem to do for both convenience and cost reasons. To us that just sounded dull and we were adamant we were going to enjoy ourselves and eat real food. Now here I was trying to lick the last drop of honey out of a single portion and not even any bloody bread to put it on. Things needed to improve and fast.

At the first opportunity we stopped for a drink and snack at a canal-side café. I've already had to admit to eating burgers from a well-known American food outlet, so I may as well also "fess up" to (for the first time in my life, as far as I am aware) actually wanting a bottle of Cola with a packet of crisps. That Cola was amazing, although it pains me to say it! The combination of salt, sugar and caffeine definitely hit the right spot. Still finding the cycle shorts tight, I also increased the size of the cuts I'd made the day before and added a few more. They now resembled something like the Incredible Hulk's trousers when he gets angry.

Refuelled, less shaky, more comfortable and spirits lifted, we were once again able to take in the beauty of the canal and the wildlife and make some sort of progress. We even found a decent-sized shop and finally managed to stock up on provisions. We went a bit overboard, and the panniers were crammed full and extremely heavy, but it was a price we were willing and happy to pay. Compared to being hungry, it seemed a doddle.

We spent a pleasant evening outside our tent on our little camp chairs cooking up a feast, and yet another cold night inside. We had already established an evening routine which worked for us. We arrived, Iain put up the tent whilst I showered (I have long hair which takes some time to dry with no hair dryer, so best to get done as soon as possible), and he put his panniers in the outer tent and his chair up. I put my panniers into the outer tent, put the bedding into the inner tent, inflated the sleep mats and wrestled them into their sheet pockets (which turned out to be a bit of a pain in the confined space), whilst Iain showered (whilst in shower we charged phone or tablet). We then hung out our towels and washed clothing (usually on our bikes). I put up my folding chair. I cooked, Iain drank wine and ate crisps. We then ate the meal and both drank wine. We washed up, checked the bikes (cleaned and oiled if necessary), and then later put the kettle on for a warm drink. We soaked our porridge overnight in apple juice (in plastic tubs with lids), so we got that ready. After a last visit to the loo block and a teeth clean, we turned in, around about 9pm.

Most nights, Iain, for reasons known only by him and maybe not even that, decided to go out again for another pee just 30 minutes after turning in. This usually meant that just as I was dropping off, he would re-enter (read fall into) the tent and manage without fail to either fall, kneel or step on me or generally bash me around the head, as he tried unsuccessfully to get in without disturbing me. Watching his lack of balance and agility and his inability to turn himself 180 degrees without resorting to contortion was my nightly comic entertainment, and I was soon looking forward, albeit slightly nervously, to each night's instalment. I labelled this nightly occurrence, much to his amusement, as his nightly inconveniences.

We still had a lot to learn about cycle touring, but with our established efficient camp routine, our panniers full of food for a change, an absence of injuries, aches and pains, and Hulk pants, we were beginning to feel a bit more confident.

For the next few days we continued without major incident to average very poor distances, and in all honesty, we were disappointed with ourselves. Surely we weren't really that unfit? With a lack of open campsites we stayed in a youth hostel in a town called Pontivy. To our surprise, we were the youngest people there. With a three-person room to ourselves, with two sinks, it was more like a hotel than a youth hostel. We took advantage of the availability of a real oven and ate a tasty lasagne accompanied by a bottle of wine at a real table on the balcony overlooking the canal, as we looked forward to a warm and decent night's sleep for a change.

During the evening under real lighting and wearing his glasses, Iain discovered that he'd set the tripometer wrongly. We were in fact not measuring our progress in kilometres but in miles. Day one of our take-it-easy training and build-it-up-gradually trip, we thought we had covered 64km (which was already clearly a few km too far), but in actual fact we'd covered 64 miles (a whopping 103km!). No wonder we were injured, knackered and were taking a few days to get over it. Perhaps this might also go some way to explain how we had a bit of trouble map reading and ended up on the BMX track down to the canal! On the plus side, it meant that we were actually bang on schedule. We had covered just over 160km in five days and were averaging our training target of 32km per day, totally accidently. After a few hours of deserved and justified mocking, morale was suitably restored.

Chapter 7
Pants

Deciding my Hulk gel pants were still too tight, I opted instead to wear my old thin foam ones. There were immediately two distinct advantages: one, the blood actually seemed to circulate around my legs whilst cycling, the skin lost that bluish tinge – surely that had to be good, and two, I didn't have to walk around feeling like I was wearing a huge nappy. For me, things were looking up and I felt as if I was getting into the swing of it all. Conversely, Iain had swapped his knee pain for an extremely swollen and tender Achilles tendon. He didn't moan but I could tell it was troubling him as he was still eating ibuprofen like Smarties and not racing off ahead quite as far as usual.

We took the advice of Yann, the manager, and fellow cyclist, at the hostel, who recommended we took the route to Nantes along the Le Blavet river as it was a slightly better surface and a much prettier route than the canal we had intended to follow. We covered a good distance, and with a warm day of perhaps more than 20 degrees, but no convenient pharmacy to confirm as such, we still managed to burn a little, despite applying sun-cream. It was, indeed a beautiful and very peaceful route. We spent our lunchtime at a weir, in our fold-out chairs munching on fine French bread, paté, cheese, tomatoes and boiled eggs, watching the fishermen. That afternoon we saw either a beaver or a coypu, not sure which, but it was lovely to see some wildlife of the mammal variety.

In France, without fail, every other cyclist we passed, whether tourer, racer, recreational or just out to get their shopping, would at the very least smile, wave and shout *bonjour*. More often than not, they would ask where have you come from? Where are you going? Whole lines of racers would greet us (some would even stop when travelling in the opposite direction) and have a genuinely interested conversation with us. If they were travelling the same way, they would slow to our speed in order to chat as we cycled, and on hills ensured that we (with the load) set the pace. They would then speed off wishing us a cheerful "*bon route*". They often seemed genuinely jealous that they weren't off on a tour of their own and were impressed by the distance that we intended to cover. When we came across other tourers, the conversation usually started with the usual, where have you come from, where are you going bit, whilst simultaneously checking out each other's bikes and kit. We would then usually give each other tips on potential camping spots, shop locations and other useful route information and wish each other luck as we got on our way. We were so impressed at how friendly and helpful all the cyclists (at this stage mostly French) we met were towards us.

Sod's law dictates that there is always an exception, and we met them that very afternoon. Ahead I spotted Iain chatting to a couple of tourers whilst waiting for me. They were a couple from Holland, a lady with panniers and a man with a single-wheel trailer. The first thing she said to me in a really brisk manner (I'm thinking the Germanic accent was responsible for this) was, "Are you annoyed with your husband being so far in front?" "Hello," I reply. "I'm Donna. Pleased to meet you. I see you have already met Iain. Where are you off to?" "We are doing many bike tours and my husband would never leave me like that, he is most responsible," she barked. "Well, we are happy, we just don't cycle at the same speed and it makes more sense—" (I was cut off mid explanation). "It is not right, you could have problems," she stated. "I would not allow it." I smiled politely, thinking, what a control freak. Iain and her partner decided sensibly to remain silent. "You are going a long way. How far do you go every day? It must be about 100km," she answered herself (I'm guessing to get the answer she wanted!). "Well no, we have six months, so we do whatever we feel like." "That is NO good, you must be more exact. And why do you have the same size bike as me? It is surely too big for you." By now I had bonded with my possibly too big bike and, feeling the need to defend Polo, I resorted to, "I don't think so. Maybe yours is too small," adding a cheery "better be off now, we have 100km to cover. Lead the way, Iain." Iain and I cycled off, him in front to prove a point, chuckling to ourselves. Somehow we didn't think the same could be said for them.

As I pulled up to my irresponsible husband (waiting patiently as ever) later in the day, I experienced a serious problem. As I put my foot to the floor, I felt a sudden excruciating pain in the coccyx region and couldn't help but cry out. The loud, low, almost cow mooing noise I made was a total surprise! Iain was worried. Once on a previous bike ride he had suffered the exact same experience (the pain, not the cow noise), so he knew how agonising it was. I was worried: it really hurt.

With miles until the next campsite, we had no option but to continue onward. I was determined not to be the reason behind another failed mission. Getting back onto the saddle was a difficult affair, but eventually, after much experimentation, I worked out that starting off from a standing position and gradually easing the bottom onto the saddle whilst keeping the legs moving was the least painful, but not totally pain-free, strategy.

I then spent my time trying to work out physiologically what was causing it, concluding that it probably had something to do with the position of my pelvis. I must have looked a complete fool as I spent hours continuously varying my pelvic position between a neutral position to either tilt my pelvis forward like Elvis or tilt it back and stick out my backside like a twerker on a bike. It appeared to make absolutely no difference. I tried sitting forward on the seat, back on the seat, balancing on one bum cheek, then the other – still no difference. Every time I stood down off the bike I would be incapacitated by a pain so serious it caused me to cry. Getting back on was becoming more and more agonising, and a non-painful seated position was proving to be more and more elusive. Maybe the Hulk nappy did do something after all? Maybe I needed a new saddle? Mine was exactly the same spec as Iain's and, unsurprisingly, we didn't have the same anatomy in that department. As I said earlier, we still had a lot to learn.

After consulting friends and family (handy Pilates instructors and osteopaths), we loosely concluded between us that it was most probably a coccyx issue, either impacted or twisted, it may or may not be helped by a few exercises (it wasn't!) and would probably be improved by a new saddle, some stronger pills and the reintroduction of the Hulk pants. Rest and time off the saddle was probably the most likely cure, but not an option. Normal pills I could do straight away, stronger we got from the pharmacy the next day. The Hulk pants were given a further trim using the teeny-tiny scissors on Iain's Leatherman (multi-purpose penknife) at the side of a road (and they now looked more like Bridget Jones' big pants with serrated edges), and we continued in search of the first convenient bike shop to buy a new saddle.

The next few days were quite honestly the most agonising and possibly most distressing days I have ever encountered. Every single lump and bump sent excruciating pain deep into my behind and lower back. When the route surface deteriorated I found myself often in tears again, and as we encountered mile upon mile of cobbles, I was back impersonating Ellen MacArthur again. It was looking increasingly likely that, although I desperately wanted to complete this challenge, it was just not going to happen.

Chapter 8
Heading east at last

Roscoff

Hills

Morlaix

Met Xavier

Fall

Fermé

Hotel

Carhaix-Plouguer

Derelict Chateaux

BMXing

Pontivy

Closed Festival

Trip-o-meter Discovery

Canal de Nantes à Brest

Yann's Detour

Met Dutch Couple

Redon

Cock-up Plan

In Plan, in Blain

Met Jacques

Nantes

Roscoff
to
Nantes

By the time we reached Nantes, it would be fair to say we felt knackered and were both often in pain. Although the days were warm, the nights were still cold and we were suffering from a definite lack of sleep. However, we were also beginning to feel like we were making some progress at last and had managed to cover almost 400km. During our conversations with fellow cyclists, our turn to answer the "where have you come from?" question with "Roscoff" wasn't quite as embarrassing as it had previously been. Nantes was the beginning of our long journey east, the start of the EuroVelo 6 route to the Black Sea. Well, if we could find it, that was. Route signs on cycle paths seem to be quite good at directing you into a town, not so good at directing you around or through the town or onto the right path to get out of town again. In cities this was even more evident, and with a multitude more roads to get lost on. And so we spent an hour, if not longer, totally lost in Nantes.

Eventually we met an older chap called Jacques (probably late 70s, maybe older) on a bike. He was visiting his son in Nantes and was out for a casual ride in his jeans and on his son's bike. As he guided us to where he thought the route was, past a few burnt-out cars, travellers' camps, dumped sofas and a fair bit of rubbish, we were slightly concerned that maybe Jacques' memory wasn't quite what it used to be! When we eventually glimpsed our first view of the river Loire we were both relieved and grateful in equal measure. Jacques then accompanied us for 26km before announcing that perhaps he should go back to his wife before she became worried. He had only popped out for a short ride and he had to get back yet! A lovely guy. When he found out how far we were planning to go, he donated a euro for each of the kilometres he had accompanied us towards our chosen charity. We promised to send him a postcard from the Black Sea when we made it. Jacques was concerned that we weren't actually wearing our cycle helmets. We reassured him that we did so when travelling on the roads. "Still," he said, staring intently at me, "even on a path, it is a long way to fall down from a big bike where you are too high."

Our first campsite experience along the EuroVelo 6 was impressive. It had an enclosed area specifically for bike tourers, with a gazebo set up, inside which were trestle tables, benches, a fridge, hotplate, microwave and a kettle, all free of charge – amazing. The pitch fee was just 14 euros too. We were the only ones on site, and were quite tempted to pitch our tent inside the gazebo for a bit of warmth, but were too respectful (read cowardly) to do so. No one else arrived, so we left our kit and pannier bags on the bikes in the gazebo overnight. As we hadn't unpacked quite so much stuff and didn't have to wait for the stove to cool down before being able to pack it away, we got going much faster than usual in the morning and, as a consequence, decided not to bother unloading our panniers into our tent each night any more. Many of the EuroVelo 6 campsites in France offered the same type of facilities for cycle tourists. They were fantastic. Some even had rooms for wet-weather sheltering, most had bike pumps with pressure gauges. They really were cycle friendly and reasonably priced.

The Diclofenac helped a lot and I had at least stopped my daytime blubbing. The weather had improved and the most significant difference was that the night-time temperature, although still not warm, was at least above zero. Unfortunately, Iain was finding his sleep mat close to useless and his hip pain was now a nightly issue, so he remained sleep deprived. Up until now, we had always felt the only way to warm up after a freezing night was to get moving and get cycling. Consequently, after cycling for eleven days straight, we had not yet had a day off the saddle – no wonder I had a sore arse!

When we stopped for lunch we had already covered a distance of 36km. Chuffed with our (pain-relief-assisted) progress, we decided to press on to the next campsite (about another 25km). The surface was good, and we were both enjoying the day and feeling no gripes. At about the 50km mark, the medication benefit ran out and my coccyx issue returned with a vengeance. The next available campsite was about another 11km, which, if it hadn't been along a potholed track interspersed with nice historic cobbled streets, wouldn't have been such an awful experience. Sensing I needed a break, Iain stopped at a lovely-looking tea room and waited for me. Rather than parking my bike into the bike-stand, all I could manage was a pain-induced partially controlled crash, once again impersonating a mooing cow. With tears streaming, I limped away from my crashed bike and the surprised onlooking tea-drinkers previously enjoying a relaxing river view, to cry and then pull myself together whilst leaning on a conveniently placed wall. Not the first time I thought that the idea of being an adventure traveller was a lot harder than I had anticipated.

With no alternative but to press on to the campsite (probably now 5km away), I tried tackling the next couple of kilometres standing up, before my knees objected to pushing 35kg of weight. Then I revisited the twerking Elvis routine – only to find the campsite was closed. Nooooooo! Iain, kindly, left me at the bus stop outside the closed campsite and went off in search of an alternative. An hour later he returned smiling (big relief). The good news was he had found a nice one, with a pool. The bad news was we had to get to the supermarket first, as we didn't have time to get pitched up before it closed, and the supermarket was about a mile uphill. We rode up – I have no idea how I made it – stocked up and then rolled downhill (thank God!) to the campsite. I couldn't cope with our usual set-up routine. I just rocked from side to side, like a woman in labour, from one foot to the other, groaning and moaning, whilst Iain set up the tent. Not a good day.

Our first rest day was definitely overdue and we were looking forward to it. Once pitched up on the campsite, more than anything else we were looking forward to not having to pack it all away again the following morning. We looked forward to that part so much that we didn't pack up the following morning either. After all, we had injuries which really needed rest to recover more than anything else, and we still had a long way and a long time to go. A couple of days relaxing in the sun, eating good food, catching up on sleep, swimming (read floating) in the pool and not sitting on a saddle did us the world of good.

Iain treated himself to a new sleeping mat. The updated version was a luxurious full centimetre thicker and was even wider than the original. Perhaps now he would be less inclined to think he needed to sleep on both of our mats and would stay on just his own. Annoyingly, it rendered half of my expertly hand-crafted sheet envelope useless. It also weighed a tonne (well over 2kg anyway!), but this was the price he was willing to pay for a night's sleep.

When we next set off, fully loaded, with both old and new mat in search of a post office (to post old one home), Solo looked more like an HGV than a touring bike.

Chapter 9
Sitting in the dark

With the new, cheap, heavy mattress getting Iain's seal of approval, the old, expensive, light one was despatched by post off to our son's house in France. After our two days off and both getting some sleep at last, we certainly felt a lot more positive.

We planned and actually managed to achieve a sensible day at last where we didn't over-extend or injure ourselves. We even stopped for a civilised picnic lunch at the troglodyte cave village of Turquant and I had time to wander around taking some photos whilst Iain took a siesta in a conveniently located covered picnic shelter. We pitched up at a reasonable time for the night on a lovely-looking 4-star campsite L'Isle Verte in a place called Montsoreau.

As I was sitting on the loo that evening, the lights went out. I tried waving about to perhaps engage a sensor and turn them back on, but nothing happened. I tried methodically feeling around the wall in my cubicle (yuck! but needs must) to perhaps a find a light switch. I found none. I had no option but to finish off in the dark (I'm not sure if you've ever had a poo in the dark in a strange place before, but I hadn't and I wouldn't want to again, it's really eerie). Wiping in the dark was interesting too and seemed to require an awful lot more concentration and was more methodical and yet more tentative compared to light-enhanced wiping. All of this was accompanied by a large dose of hope for the best and followed by rigorous hand-washing. Note to self and anyone else planning this type of trip: always wear a head torch to the toilet block, even if it's light when you enter. Needless to say, Iain found my toilet antics amusing.

We didn't sleep well. Again, it was a cold night, and for some reason at 2am we were woken by door-slamming and banging noises coming from the toilet block, at 6am by relentless traffic noise, then again at about 6.45am by shouting and arguing. From what we could decipher from the French argument, a gentleman had been in the shower last night (at 2am?) when suddenly the lights went out (familiar), and because it was dark, he was unable to turn the shower temperature up and had instead turned it down and it was now freezing. He then couldn't work out how to get out of the cubicle. He did eventually but then tripped over the *raclette* (scraper to dry floor off with) and fell against another door and into another cubicle. Oops, and I thought I'd had trouble! With no satisfactory response from the campsite owner, Monsieur Douche got into his campervan and revved off site, still purple in the face and threatening legal action.

I possessed neither the appropriate language skills nor the desire to further upset the campsite owner by relaying my own inconvenient lack-of-light moment. I think he had had enough. With an early start and finally managing to get our morning pack-up routine down to about an hour and twenty minutes, we were on the road by 8.30am, which was a record for us.

After about 30km, the coccyx pain restarted, nicely coinciding with a sign warning us of uneven surface for the next 2km. Shit. (Diary *verbatim*: "RETURN OF THE KILLER COCCYX PAIN – UNEVEN SURFACE SIGN – FOR FUCKS SAKE!!!!").

When we came across an unexpected small bike-hire shop (not marked on the route map), it was such a relief. Just for a change, I could have cried. I went in and bought the fattest, widest, most cushioned girly round-bottom-shaped, with integral suspension ladies' saddle they had in stock and prayed that it would make a difference. I honestly didn't think I would be able to take much more if it didn't.

It turns out that most people who know what they are doing on a bike know that a bike is sold with a standard generic saddle. It is assumed that, with so many specialist saddles, and so many different-shaped people, people who know what they are doing will go out and immediately buy (or already possess) a saddle which specifically suits them. We didn't know this. We do now and learnt the hard way. Maybe the fact that both Iain's and my bike had identical saddles on them and our behinds are in no way similar should have made alarm bells ring? Maybe I just didn't want to admit to needing a wider saddle as that would mean finally admitting I do have a wider arse than I'd like! I'm over that now. I'd rather accept the truth than be subjected to excruciating butt pain for even a second longer. At a later date, Iain also ended up replacing his to reduce compression on a nerve, which was causing some numbness.

The new saddle and the timing seemed like a miracle. We managed another 28km without pain, tears or even swearing as we entered into beautiful chateau territory. That evening we were treated to not just an outdoor heated swimming pool but a fully functioning fantastic Jacuzzi. Boy, did we get those powerful jets positioned onto all the achy bits. Things were really looking up.

The temperature continued to rise the next day. As usual, we were reliably informed by the pharmacy signs mid-morning that it was 32°C, and later in the day that it was 37°C. You get a lot of time to wonder and ponder things on a bike, when not distracted by pain, that is. I wondered why pharmacies in France nearly always have a large green neon temperature display. Perhaps, I pondered, it drummed up business in some way? Did French people see the sign and immediately think, "oh my goodness, I didn't realise it was that hot, I'd better stock up on heat-reducing remedies." Or "wow, look how cold it is. I had no idea. Well, that settles it, I'd better rush in now quickly, before the two-hour-lunch closing time, and buy some extra warming tablets." Perhaps the only people really finding them useful was us, as we had chosen, perhaps wrongly, not to take a thermometer for weight restriction reasons. It certainly wasn't essential to know the temperature (because, funnily enough, we could actually feel how hot or cold we were) whilst on the trip, but it has become useful in the telling of these tales and the accuracy of them, otherwise I could have quite easily succumbed to wild exaggerations and you would be none the wiser.

We were a little sunburnt, despite the pharmacy warning signs, when we stopped for the night at the lovely medieval town of Amboise, and we had time to treat ourselves to an ice cream overlooking Chateau du Clos Luci. With the good weather forecast to continue and our many ailments under control, we enjoyed a fabulous relaxed evening of good camp-cooked food (obligatory crisps, olives and *saucisson* to start, prawns in a crème fraiche and shallot sauce with pasta and salad, dark chocolate for dessert). And, of course, seeing as we were in chateau country, a bottle of wine was obligatory.

As we approached the beautiful town of Blois the following day, Iain's Achilles problem was becoming more of an issue and it was now twice the width of the other one. We decided we would stop early for the day, stay in a youth hostel and spend an evening in the bustle of a town for a change. We followed signs to the tourist office, up the hill, then up some steps, then up another hill, all the while wondering "what type of logical explanation could be behind putting the bloody tourist office at the top, and not the bottom, of a pedestrianised hill?" To add insult to, admittedly already collected, injury, they informed us there was no longer a youth hostel in town, though there were two 5km away in the opposite directions to our route. The nearest campsites were 18km and 20km further along but were at least on route. The tourist information centre called but neither was open for the season yet. Luckily, the one at 22km was, so we reserved a pitch in advance. With our plan for an evening of townie castle culture scuppered, but at least in the knowledge that we would be able to stop in less than a couple of hours, we enjoyed a rare freewheel back down the hill.

We decided not to honour our pitch agreement at 22km as it was absolutely jam-packed full of travellers (modern caravans with modern cars, not romantic wooden ones with horses). I'm sure it would most probably have been safe, but we didn't really want to risk having our bikes or their wheels nicked, although, with hindsight, I'm sure that as we didn't have anything with a Mercedes badge on, we would have been fine. Without either bikes or wheels our trip would have been over and we didn't want to risk it. Instead we carried on to the next available campsite on route and, truly knackered, stopped after a gruelling 82km. Once again, not what we'd really planned or envisaged when we set out for the day.

We were the only people on site. After we pitched up we were informed that the only shower block in use was the one at the far end, only a kilometre away. Yippee. We decided to ride to the shower block that evening. It was great as the hot water wasn't limited by push buttons, it was clean and, as a bonus, it was even fully lit. That evening as I was sitting quietly preparing dinner, I was startled by Iain as he crashed through the hedge, looking seriously knackered and stressed, onto our pitch carrying his bike! Whilst I thought he had been enjoying a long leisurely shower, he had in fact lost his bike key (they have integral locks which stop the wheel from turning) and had spent the last 40 minutes crawling around the shower cubicle and in the grass around the bike looking for the key. Convinced he had lost it down a drain, he had carried his bike back the full kilometre to the pitch to dig out the spare key. Within seconds, I found the key in his shorts pocket that he had already searched through, in proper man fashion, several times. My turn to be amused by his antics.

For the next few days an irritating repetitive routine seemed to occur. Anything interesting, useful or essential to visit would always be off-route and at the top of a hill. All of the municipal campsites that looked to be the perfect distance on the map turned out to be full of travellers. As a consequence, we always seemed to be going further than we would have liked to, but at least we were beginning to feel fitter and more able to do so.

That was until the wind decided to rear its head again and the temperature plummeted.

Chapter 10
Earth, wind and fire

Maybe I should apologise? I have focused far more on the difficulties and pain we endured and the whingeing that I did than anything else. Maybe I shouldn't apologise? That's just how it was in the early days; it was no picnic. In fact, no! I shouldn't. During (what became known as) the Nuclear Pikey Valley stage of our beautiful Loire valley tour, we endured not only a lack of lovely scenery but (diary entry *verbatim*) "a freezing cold head-wind from hell, all f***ing day, except when it was instead intent on blowing us sideways off of a bridge." I had now picked up a cold and was having difficulty breathing or maintaining a sensible temperature. Feeling alternately cold and hot resulted in several days of fleece on, fleece off annoyance and never really feeling comfortable. The combination of illness and head-wind meant a day of maximum exertion for very little reward. At times the bike actually remained static, despite putting intense effort into pedal pushing. Our weariness was evident when, once again, our chosen campsite was fully occupied by gypsies. After much toil, we reached a suitable alternative, having covered 72km.

Two more days of head-wind, colder temperatures and illness followed. I finally relented and bought a sleeping bag. I was determined it would squeeze somehow into the panniers. Binning my pride and joy home-made sheet envelope (no longer any use since the arrival of Iain's new sleep mat) helped, but the fact the sleeping bag was a child's one and only 4.5ft long probably had more to do with its space-saving qualities. At last I experienced my first truly snug, warm and comfortable night's sleep. I wished I had thought of it earlier. I tried to encourage Iain to get one too, but he insisted he was now comfortable, and besides, a 4.5ft-long bag wasn't going to be much use to him, so he bought a cotton sleeping-bag liner instead, which he sensibly pointed out was probably going to be more use than my bag when and if it did finally get hot.

I was hoping to sleep late into the morning of our next day off, at a campsite near another nuclear power station, in Sully des Loire, when I was woken suddenly by a loud unidentifiable noise. I called out to Iain. No reply. I poked my head out of the tent and saw a huge billowing cloud of dark, dense smoke rising from behind the hedge adjacent to our tent. Towards the smoke-filled area a spectacled man, who was not naturally gifted with the build of a runner, was attempting to run along the river path and onto the site. Gasping for breath and sweating profusely, he emerged from behind the hedge and proceeded to drag a huge (size of a large Labrador dog) charred metallic object back towards the river path. A minute or two later, the campsite owner arrived and, pointed in the right direction by Iain, he pursued the sweaty spectacled man. In the meantime, the smoke tower had encouraged everyone from within a 2km radius to congregate behind the hedge and have a long and detailed conversation about the incident. It was widely agreed by the masses that the police should be called as this "could be a matter of national security being near to the nuclear power station". The owner returned and confirmed that actually "yes, the police should be called because the man was a pervert." He had been trying to take photographs of the unroofed toilet and shower block. Iain had watched the drone as it had gone higher and higher. Just as he wondered what would happen if it went out of range, it just fell out of the sky at tremendous speed. It crashed heavily, causing a large dent in the tarmac, and simultaneously the battery had caught fire. Thankfully, it landed between two caravans and the hedge which separated our tent from them and not on me or anyone else.

With lie-in definitely ruined, we headed into town for supplies and to have a look at Chateau Sully. So far we had managed to see the outside of many chateaux but the inside of none. In the castle grounds we spotted some other cycle tourers. With a mountain of equipment, fluorescent warning signs, warning triangles, thousands of reflectors, many flags and the fact we could hear them speaking from what must have been more than 100 metres away, there was no mistaking that they were Americans.

We introduced ourselves and, after a reasonable bit of deserved banter following their comment on how pleased they were to finally find someone else who spoke their language, we immediately warmed to them. The dreaded head-wind was discussed in detail; they too were finding it an unpleasant challenge. Crazy Harry and his friend (not partner) Johnny were also heading to the Black Sea despite Harry having two replacement hips due to arthritis and recovering from his second heart attack just a few weeks before. They were pressing on that day, but we arranged to meet at Sancerre on their next scheduled rest day for a spot of wine tasting. They were surprised that both of our bikes were much bigger than theirs, despite one of them being of taller-than-average height. Harry also was convinced that I would need to be changing both my bike as "too big" and definitely my (new) saddle as he thought it was "far too wide and impractical to be suitable for long-distance touring". Seeing as he had no idea of my old saddle problems, just what would he, and his American male behind, know about that? I thought.

Cooking dinner that evening proved to be a bit of a palaver. The wind was still strong, despite using our small metal windbreak, so the burner flame, instead of being useful and heading up towards the saucepans, was being blown sideways onto the table. Not only did it take much longer than usual to cook anything due to flame direction issues but we also had to refuel several times during the cooking (not usually necessary) because the fuel was burning faster than usual. To make matters even more of a commotion, we also managed to set fire to the picnic bench three times!

We set off again along the featureless levies, with the Loire hardly ever in view, and once again accompanied by the dreaded head-wind. Not what you'd call the most interesting, attractive or fun section, so when our maps offered an alternative route along a canal, we were instantly in agreement to take it. After we had cycled over an impressive aqueduct, the scenery became more interesting, with beautiful tree-lined paths, copious wild flowers, lilies on the canal, plenty of heron-type birds and, most significantly, the head-wind became almost non-existent. We now even had boats to look at. Apart from a handful of vintage flat-bottomed barges, mostly now permanently moored and used as holiday accommodation, we noticed that despite being a huge river, the Loire seemed almost entirely devoid of boat traffic, which surprised us.

Again we were subjected to the non-existence of an actual campsite marked clearly on our map. Consequently, once again we ended up covering more distance than we would have liked. At least on this occasion we were compensated by coming across a real existing campsite (which was not even hinted at on the map), much closer than the no-doubt non-existing next one marked on the map. It cost just 7 euros for us both and had the most pleasant shower block we had encountered to date, we were happy campers.

We continued accompanied by countless herons or maybe cranes, some grey, some black and white (I'm no bird expert). They would be standing totally upright on low branches at the water's edge, as still as statues, presumably waiting patiently for unsuspecting passing fish.

As we approached, they would open their enormous wings, take off and fly silently alongside us, looking ungainly with head and neck at an odd angle, like creatures from a bygone era, until they found another suitable fishing spot. Beside us the banks were bursting with spring flowers in purple, pink, white and yellow, and we experienced a pleasant, warm, wind-free and relaxing ride into Sancerre. We also passed and chatted with a French couple on the way to Budapest on touring bikes with a Heath Robinson-type contraption extending from the handlebars which allowed their two dogs to be on leads but run along with them. They were towing a trailer, mostly full of dog paraphernalia, and were going incredibly slowly.

Sancerre is a hilltop medieval and Roman town famous for both wine and goat's cheese. Luckily for us, the campsite was by the river and not in town. We arrived early, keen to get to town and have a look around. Our early (3pm) was too late for the last bus up to town. The campsite owner informed us it was either an hour's walk up or a heck of a bike ride up, up and up some more; she wouldn't want to do it. Luckily, one of her staff was going to the shops and would be able to give us a lift up and we could get a taxi back. It was worth the visit. After a couple of hours of wandering around old streets, the purchasing of a suitable gift for the campsite ladies and a couple of blocks of goat's cheese and a bottle of wine, we relished the amazing view over the river Loire and the surrounding vineyards from the top of town whilst we waited for our 11 euro taxi journey back to the campsite.

Back on site we found our American friends, Crazy Harry and Johnny. They had been out wine tasting all day and Crazy Harry was already looking a little worse for wear. We started the evening off on site with goat's cheese, crackers and crisps, and we had three bottles of wine to "taste" before heading off to a restaurant within walking distance. The first bottle had been gifted to Johnny, who had come across a fellow cyclist on the cycle route. He had said, "call in to my shop in Sancerre, I own a vineyard," and, true to his word, and totally unbelievable to the Americans, a free bottle with Johnny's name was indeed waiting for him. The second was bought by Harry (having just sold his own vineyard in California, he knew his wine). Ours was a red, because that's what we prefer, especially without a fridge. And so commenced an evening of high alcohol consumption. In our defence, you can't carry wine easily on a bike, you have to drink it, and they were all too nice to sample and spit or not finish the bottle. You expect a person known as "Crazy" to become more and more animated and, true to form, this was the case, particularly when he found out the same taxi journey had just cost them four times the amount it had cost us. He was entertaining and we got on well, but we didn't really get the chance to find out much about Johnny, other than he was a bike tour veteran on the American continent, he wrote a bike blog and was accompanying Crazy Harry. As we were all heading the same way, we were likely to encounter them again. Maybe next time it would be best to at least start the meal sober! Still, it was a welcome change for us to eat out, stay up later than 9pm and have someone else entertain us.

With five days of heavy rain forecast, we opted to take a mini-break and give our injuries a rest and the chance to recover properly. The camp manager let us store our luggage in an empty caravan free of charge, and with the bikes locked up in a Porta cabin, we set off by train to visit our son in the sunny south of France. It was raining there too!

Chapter 11
On a roll

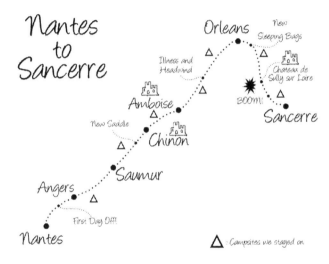

Nantes
to
Sancerre

Orleans

New
Sleeping Bags

Illness and
Headwind

Amboise

Chateau de
Sully sur Loire

New Saddle

Chinon

300mi!

Sancerre

Saumur

Angers

First Day Off!

Nantes

△ : Campsites we stayed on

We returned from our rainy mini-break fully refreshed and eager to get going again. We arrived back at the campsite late afternoon instead of early afternoon due to wrongly getting off the train at the furthest away of the two Sancerre stations (ironically this was the one the staff had given us a lift to on the way out!). We then had to wait in order to get a train back again and, in the absence of any taxis, of which there were an abundance at the other station, we had to walk the couple of kilometres back to site. All of which meant we had to grudgingly pitch for the night instead of setting straight off.

With a slight improvement in the nocturnal temperature, Iain decided he no longer needed to wear his merino wool leggings at night. He only remembered this costume change halfway through the night about midway between the tent and toilet block, as he "felt a little more breezy than usual around the balls". He emerged back into the tent apparently unnoticed by any fellow campers, and for the second time that day, in fits of laughter. Previously the same evening he had also forgotten that the men's toilet block was closed and he was supposed to use the female block. On this occasion it was the lack of toilet roll which brought the mistake to his attention. Luckily, the water wasn't switched off, so he could at least flush away the evidence. He then spent almost an hour listening for silence in order to ascertain the perfect moment to make a break for it. With a naked, unwiped bottom, his thighs as far akimbo as is humanly possible, and with trousers around the ankles, he somehow managed to shuffle to the other block without being noticed. How he got away with that, I'll never know.

On our very first day back cycling, it was still raining and we re-overtook the French couple with the two, now very wet, dogs. After establishing that they too hadn't taken a few days off, we concluded that they probably wouldn't even get to Nevers 76km away any time soon, let alone Budapest, not unless they extended their trip by a couple of years.

We were now into a good routine, since the new saddle and the break we could both cycle further without pain or reigniting injuries, and it felt good. This was also just as well seeing as many of the campsites were still either closed for the season, closed permanently years ago or were occupied by gypsies, which added extra mileage to the end of most days. We now felt more confident about physically being able to make the distance. At 11am on the 1st of May at Eclise de Roche on the Canal du Nivernais, after less than a month away (including our mini-break), we reached the 1,000km mark and celebrated in the drizzle with an extravagant sip of water and a fruitcake bar.

Almost everything about camping required extra effort when raining. Putting away the wet tent meant carrying a heavier tent. Putting up a wet tent meant wiping the inside and waiting for it to dry out before being able put anything into it. We took a tarpaulin (tarp) along with us for cooking and sitting under in bad weather, and this turned out to be exceptionally useful. But of course, this had to be rigged up, put away, and was also heavier to carry when wet. It was almost impossible for us to get towels and washing dry – even when draped over the bikes under the tarp for the night they were still a bit damp in the morning. Packing things into and out of the panniers without getting water in was quite an art, not necessarily one that was mastered either. We had waterproof saddle covers, which proved to be useless, so they were binned. Probably the most annoying bit of kit failure was my expensive waterproof coat, which actually ended up on every occasion wetter inside than it was on the outside. I seriously thought I would have been better off wearing a bin bag.

Campsites with extra facilities for cyclists were like an oasis in bad weather. As we entered a designated cyclist room on one site, we were greeted by a friendly German man, first in French, then English, once we all realised none of us were French or actually possessed any talent at speaking it. He was surrounded by lines of drying washing, towels, shoes, tables full of maps, food, drinks, charging phones and gadgets, and a hotplate of pasta bubbling away and a kettle on the boil. We then got to meet Lorenz's wife Ziggy and their two children, three-year-old Freddie and almost one-year-old Laura. They were travelling on their specialised tandem from Spain back home to Germany with the kids in a bike trailer, camping all the way and they were enjoying every minute of it. We spent a fantastic evening and shared a cobbled-together meal with them. Their command of the English language and even knowledge of English politics was probably greater than most of the people we know. We arranged to meet up further along the route.

We set off the following day in torrential rain. At lunchtime we stopped to dry off in a café and decided a large hot meal would raise the spirits. It did the trick whilst still inside, but going back out in the rain again didn't seem so attractive, and cycling on a full stomach wasn't wonderful either, even if we did get to taste the lasagne again and again. Still, we managed 60km or so and by now we were not surprised to find the campsite signs saying *fermé* yet again. Luckily, the owner spotted us and, just as we were about to cycle off, he appeared, explaining, to our relief, that he had opened yesterday, but he just hadn't yet changed the sign. This time the site had handy little round picnic benches with waterproof umbrellas on each pitch. We attached our tarpaulin around the edges and made ourselves a nifty little windproof and waterproof kitchen-dining room for the evening. Studying the map and weather forecast that evening, we decided to break free from the EuroVelo 6 route the following day and take a more direct road route as it was straighter; meandering around scenic, winding routes didn't have quite so much appeal in the peeing rain.

Wet, heavy and with it still raining the next day, we joined the road, which was indeed straight for miles, probably Roman, we surmised. It most definitely was not flat, though, and we were faced with a serious series of nine or ten really long and fairly steep hills. This alternative route certainly didn't look likely to gain us any advantage. With not even a bend in sight, we could see the full length and severity of every challenging hill before we even started, which somehow seemed to make it worse. It was a hard day, but when comparing our capabilities on the first much, much shorter hills in the beginning near Roscoff, our performance was a huge improvement; we were like different cyclists, almost professional in fact. We could breathe, were no longer beetroot red in the head, more a respectable shade of pink, and I didn't have to stop mid-hill even once.

We did stop, however, for another ill-advised long lunch in the small village of Paray le Monial, during which a group of leisure bikers arrived, clad in a variety of clothing fashioned from bin bags, shoe wraps, coats, overskirts and hats. I knew it, they were all drier on the inside than I was! After the meal, we got chatting, then whilst drinking hot chocolate and coffee, we decided to treat ourselves and booked into a hotel room for the night.

Once we had hung out almost the entire contents of our panniers, including our tent, on every conceivable coat hanger, hook, surface, towel and curtain rail, we agreed it would be much more pleasant trying to use the wi-fi in the comfort of the bar rather than in the only corner of the room facing the wall where it worked. The only guests in the hotel, we wandered down to find the door from inside the hotel to the bar was locked. We knocked, we called out, but no one was about. A bit concerning was that the door to the outside world was also locked. We established a window which we could escape from if necessary. Until the following morning at breakfast, we were to be confined within our own private Chinese laundry. A bit disgruntled at not being informed of the lack of forthcoming facilities and lack of wi-fi, being locked in and treated like naughty kids seemed to make us act accordingly. With a bit of searching, Iain found the cellar door open. They won't miss one, he thought, as he helped himself. Luckily, we had cheese, biscuits and a corkscrew with us, and our evening turned out to be not so bad after all.

From the shower the next morning came a right commotion, crashing, swearing. Rushing into the bathroom, I saw Iain clambering to an upright position and established that he had slipped, fallen and had hurt his toe. Thank goodness, I thought, as it had sounded much more serious and I had imagined broken legs or replacement hips. He dried himself off and limped out into the bedroom. Yep, his toe looked broken, swollen to twice the size, and already a stunning shade reminiscent of last night's deep red wine. Maybe it was wine karma, I suggested, which didn't go down too well, as he correctly retorted with "well you drank it too". There's not really a lot you can do for a broken toe, even if you do get it X-rayed, so he decided not to bother. Food seemed more important right then. So, I walked and Iain hobbled, without shoes on as too painful, down to breakfast to pay for the pilfered wine, just in case, and to decide what to do next.

Chapter 12
Le van man

The rain had eased off slightly and Iain, once he had managed to get his shoe on, discovered that cycling on a broken toe was, even if not totally pain-free, easier than walking on it. Well, that was lucky then!

That night we opted to head for a campsite which was 4km off-route, only to confirm (as if we still needed to) that our maps were totally useless as well as out of date, and the site had closed over five years ago. So not only did we cycle down and up two really long, steep and busy hills to get to nowhere, but we then had to cycle up and down the same very long, steep and busy hills to return to where we had started from. We vowed never to go more than a mile off-route ever again, unless absolutely essential, as it was more demoralising somehow to retrace even 4km than to have to press on and to cover an additional 30km. I guess this is more to do with knowing you are making progress in the right direction.

After 80km we still hadn't found a campsite and cheekily asked if we could put up our tent in the grounds of a private chateau (advertising chambres d'hôtes at 85 euros per person). With permission granted to set up in front of the gite, for just 10 euros, we had the use of an open barn to store the bikes, cook and shelter from the drizzle. We were given the key to use the bathroom facilities in the gite and spent some considerable time soaking in the bath – pure luxury. That evening, the chateau owner kindly brought us over a welcome gift of home-grown salad and freshly hardboiled eggs and then gave us a tour of the gardens.

Squashing a slug in my shoe with a bare foot was not the most pleasant way start to the day. Then we found our pannier bags and our tent were covered in slugs on the outside and, more disturbingly, the pannier bags were covered in slugs on the inside too. Our getting ready to set off routine now took even longer and involved removing every item from every bag, removing slugs and wiping away slimy slug trails. Eventually, very late, we set off and waved goodbye the chateau owner. He waved us over and produced a glass of red wine each to wish us *bonne route*, which wasn't quite so welcome. But with no discreet opportunity to tip it away in his presence, we had little option but to join him and set off even later.

The whole path was covered in herds of slugs (I don't know what the collective noun for a group of slugs is, but they were definitely travelling in packs and all going in the same direction). Initially we tried to avoid them, mostly to avoid sliming up the bikes, but eventually it proved to be impossible to do so. Other than the slugs, the cycling was uneventful and the weather drizzly. We stopped at another campsite where we met up with the German family again, and on this occasion they made us a delicious German soup, which we all ate crowded, against the drizzle, under our tarp.

The cycle route east from there offered two options. Our new German friends, with their HGV (tandem and trailer) decided sensibly to take the flatter riverside route. We chose the more hilly but scenic route through the vineyards. We arranged to meet again sometime before they changed direction and started to head north up the Rhine.

Our route was indeed more challenging but achievable and the scenery was well worth the effort. This was our first experience of the type of scenery we had wrongly expected to see along the whole length of the Loire. We were now cycling amongst mile upon mile of rolling hills covered in vineyards just beginning to bud, and it was beautiful with far-reaching views. Following *voies vertes* (France's quiet, bike-friendly road routes), we were relaxed, once again accompanied by sunshine, enjoying ourselves and making good progress. Iain was ahead as usual and was particularly enjoying the fun of the fast downhill sections of the rolling hills. These roads were narrow. Maybe at a push two Smart cars or original-sized Minis could pass, but not two normal-sized cars; one would have to wait in the regular pull-ins for the other to pass. But they are not busy and we only saw a couple of cars all day. On *voies vertes* I believe cyclists are supposed to be given priority, or if not priority, then respect, for example by passing a cyclist wide and slow. In most places along these lanes it was possible for a car to pass a cyclist (even a fully laden or very fat one) with no problem.

Ahead I could see Iain passing a small yellow van. With the van wheels just onto the grass verge, they both had just enough room to pass by comfortably. For some unknown reason, when the van drew level with me, the driver suddenly decided he needed to pull further over onto the verge (the road was no narrower there than where Iain had passed him). In doing so, his right-hand-side car wheels dropped into a ditch and he started shouting at me through his open window. Not exactly sure what he was saying, but recognising a few of the words on the bluer end of the spectrum and noticing his angry face, I raised my hand in a thank-you or sorry-type gesture and decided to keep cycling. The next thing I heard was a reversing van and, thinking he was just trying to get out of the ditch, I was not concerned. Then I heard the distinctive whirring sound of a car reversing, very fast. As I looked into my mirror, all I could see in the centre of a huge cloud of dust was the yellow van reversing at full speed towards me. Initially thinking he was just trying to spook me, or prove some type of ridiculous point, I was not too worried. After a few more seconds I was, though, as he was still coming after me and at full-speed reverse. I have never cycled so fast in my life. All the time I could hear the van gaining on me. Every second that passed I was hoping that he would give up his pointless scaremongering but I was becoming increasingly worried that he was actually intending on deliberately knocking me off my bike. I started shouting to Iain, hoping that at least he would see the incident and be around to patch me up in the messy aftermath. Iain is deaf; he carried on oblivious. Pedalling faster and shouting louder, still no response, but at least I hadn't been caught yet. I considered swerving in amongst the vineyards, as I figured that at least his car couldn't follow me in there, but decided that, at this speed, the change in surface could see me thrown off the bike and potentially under his wheels anyway. Just as I was seriously considering a high-pitched full-on girly scream, Iain stopped and, with no sense of urgency, turned around. (Apparently, he thought he might have heard me shout and thought he might have left one of his bags open, so had stopped to check.) I don't think he could quite believe what he was seeing – me cycling hell for leather being chased in reverse by a yellow van. As if suddenly changing from ordinary but slightly deaf human to super-bike man, he began to cycle rapidly towards me. Le Van Man stopped within a metre of hitting me and, seeing Iain on his way up the hill (why are there always hills in the most inconvenient places?), started shouting verbal abuse and waving his fists at me. Iain arrived and let the man know, without manhandling him, in no uncertain terms even with a language barrier, that if he so much as even touched his wife he would be a dead man. In twenty-five years of marriage I had never known Iain threaten anyone before.

Clearly stinking of alcohol (him not us on this occasion), we chucked in a French colloquialism for drunk along with the word *gendarmes* and proceeded to get out our telephone. For some ridiculous reason, I got out my notebook and a pen and pretended to write down his number plate. (I'm blaming shock!) With hindsight, I wish I'd got out the camera even if only to humiliate him on social media or similar. Le Van Man got back in his van, and after a painstakingly slow nine-point turn, presumably to carefully avoid any unseen ditches, he screeched off in a cloud of dust. What an arsehole.

For the next hour or so I couldn't stop my legs shaking like jelly. We stopped for a fortifying coffee in a beautiful town called Beaunne and then couldn't find our way out again. The same thing happened in St Jean de Noix. After passing yet another two closed campsites, we racked up an impressive 91km, and that included a car chase.

Chapter 13
Out of France

As we approached the town of Besancon we panicked a little. Perched up extremely high on an impressive cliff sat a collection of old buildings. We had booked into a small hotel with a BBC news channel in the old part of town to coincide with both the UK general election and our first day out of the saddle in nine days. It looked like the old part of town was not just up the regular hill that we had become accustomed to, but reaching it was going to be more like a mountain expedition. Our relief was immense when, as we got closer and rode around the bend in the river path, we realised that the town itself was at river level and it was the Citadel that was perched high up on the imposing cliffs.

The words "I'm cock a hoot" (not hoop!) and "chipper" actually came out of Iain's mouth when describing his excitement at unexpectedly being able to follow the general election on the TV. I have never heard him use either expression before and can only assume it was a mixture of the heady relief of not having to cycle up a mountain after all mixed with terminology used in a bygone era of BBC political coverage. Not that cycling day in and day out makes you mad, but it did seem to change our perspective; what we might previously have taken for granted or have considered to be mundane seemed to take on more significance.

It was lovely to have an evening meal out and have a break from the camping routine. Political predictions were mostly of the view that the Conservatives were unlikely to get in or gain a majority of the vote. We woke in the morning to learn Cameron (Conservatives) had won outright, so the end of the current coalition government. That day pretty much everyone else resigned: Miliband – Labour, Clegg – Lib Dem, Farage – UKIP. And the Scottish National Party took fifty-six of the fifty-nine Scottish seats. With it all so clear-cut, there were no aftermath power struggles to be fought or coalition deals to be announced, and the news coverage soon became dull and uninteresting. I decided to take a Nordic Walk up to the top of the Citadel.

I am a big Nordic Walking enthusiast. I set up a local community Nordic Walking project. As part of our cycle challenge I promised my Nordic Walking groups that I would be taking a Nordic Walk in every one of the countries we visited. This was in recognition of the fact that whilst I was away they were all continuing to meet, walk and donate all of their usual walk fees to the charity we were raising money for. They were a wonderful group, who not only did their regular walks but also held additional sponsored walks, took part in a fancy-dress walk before we left, and even held car boot sales. In the tough times it was certainly helpful to know they were all really rooting for our success and to see our charity total regularly rising because of their efforts. The Nordic Walking poles that I lugged around, strapped to my rear pannier rack, also came in handy for assembling our wet-weather tarp shelter. We were also informed (by one half of another UK touring couple) that they would be useful for any encounters where we needed to defend ourselves against wild dogs! The above-mentioned cyclist happened to be carrying a large, heavy metal bar for just such an occasion; she was so convinced she would need it in Romania that she was carrying it all the way across the rest of Europe – just in case.

Apart from the Citadel, everything else in Besancon was closed for a bank holiday. Apparently, France gets a bank holiday to celebrate VE day. Funny how we don't get one in the UK, I wondered. I spent a good few hours in the Citadel, an amazing feat of 17th-century engineering and a UNESCO world heritage site complete with towers and ramparts to walk around. It had an eclectic mix of displays, including beautifully preserved buildings, a well hundreds of metres deep with reinforced bomb-proof roof, a loud, colour-clashing rather spooky puppet exhibition, a Second World War Resistance Museum (which was fascinating and huge), and a rather sad and awful zoo with small enclosures housing lions, tigers and kangaroos. Apart from the zoo, I enjoyed my visit and the views of the surrounding city and countryside were incredible. Iain spent the morning, no doubt cock a hoop, in the hotel, preferring to listen to the news and make the most of an internet opportunity.

The hotel stopover gave us the usual opportunity to get some laundry done. We also sorted through our kit and packaged up some unused items to send back home. This would give us a bit more space to carry food, which would be more useful. It would appear that posting items within France is quite reasonable, but to send items abroad costs a fortune, and we were charged the equivalent of £40 to post home a few items probably not worth much more than the postage cost.

Mulhouse was the last French town on our journey. The cycle paths on the way in were busy and full of leisure cyclists, and it was a nice atmosphere on a beautiful sunny day. We spent one last fun evening with the German family before they headed north. By now it was Iain's turn to need a new saddle, due to numbness and the start of chafing (in case you are wondering). We also decided to change our tent. Our current expensive tent had a large porch. We no longer used the porch for storage, we never sat inside it as we preferred the tarp, and it also had a terrible condensation issue. Every morning, regardless of outside weather conditions, it would drip on us as we clambered out of the sleeping compartment. We bought a cheap tent with a separate entrance for each of us (marking the end of the nightly inconveniences), and we now each had a small porch for personal items and shoes. We posted our old one back to an address in France this time! Our new tent had a much more spacious sleeping compartment, more head room, packed smaller, weighed less and cost less than quarter of the price, and was easier and quicker to erect. We named it the Tardis.

The 12th of May, a momentous day, we crossed the border out of France and into Switzerland. We had crossed the country with the largest land mass of the entire trip. It certainly felt like we were making progress. It was an extremely hot day (36°C), and we were planning to stop in Basel at about 3pm to have a look around. Not for the first time, the map misinformed us. There was no campsite where indicated, and after a hectic and hair-raising ride amongst bustling traffic, an insane number of trams and throngs of people, we found the tourist office, who confirmed the lack of campsite. With the cheapest alternative being a hostel sharing a room with ten others costing more than 100CHF each, we decided to press on instead. We were disappointed as it looked like an amazing city to explore. Perhaps, when richer, we will make another visit. Thinking our maps could be no more inaccurate, after much confusion, we then discovered the actual marked route was on the opposite side of the river to where shown on the map. No wonder we couldn't find the route markers.

Finally, at about 7pm, we pulled onto our first Swiss campsite and, desperate for a good feed, we waited outwardly patiently but with internal starving impatience, whilst the campsite owner directed us to sit in his caravan awning whilst he filled out in triplicate a huge set of forms for our night's stay, including copying our entire passport details. After half an hour, thinking we were finally going to be released and could go and find some food, he showed us to the area of grass for camping and then proceeded to give us the slowest personal tour of the facilities humanly possible. I'm sure we could have worked it out for ourselves – big building with picture of shower on the door with a picture of a lady, you get the kind of thing. Thankfully, the new tent was set up in a jiffy and finally we were able to cycle off to town in search of some food.

Chapter 14
Bordering Switzerland

Over the next five days we covered 358km, often having trouble locating the route markers and becoming increasingly frustrated with our map. Why is it, we wondered, that every time we get lost or go off-route it involves going up an unnecessary hill? During this section we ended up on an extremely busy and particularly long (about 3km) bypass. With lorries and cars speeding noisily past, it was exceedingly unnerving. Although most trucks did seem to pass with some consideration, it was still difficult not to be sucked in by their airstream towards their huge wheels. Most cars bothered to pass neither wide nor slow, so brought their own hazards. It was tiring, not only because of the weight we were carrying uphill, and the additional effort required to keep the bike upright and on a straight path, but also because when you are more anxious and nervous and want to get out of the situation as quickly as possible, there is a tendency to cycle faster than usual. On this type of section we chose to cycle together; this time Iain would cycle just behind and slightly to my side, as we figured two bikes and two sets of bike lights would be more visible to the traffic approaching from behind, and should we be unfortunate enough to be involved in an accident, we would either do so together or help the other one out if not involved.

Pleased to be back on the official route again, I was then challenged by a series of extremely short, steep inclines. My difficulty was not having enough body weight, even when approaching them at full speed ahead, to counteract the combined weight of bike and luggage. Although I did get better at it, almost without fail, the bike would stop before the top and I'd have to jump off quickly in order to prevent it from toppling over to one side. On more than one occasion it brought tears to my eyes as parts of my more delicate anatomy (located between my legs) came into forcible contact with the crossbar of the bike, despite it being a bike for ladies. Bloody bike's too big, I thought.

We continued, in hot and humid weather, to cross into and out of Switzerland and Germany, now following the Rhine river, never really sure which country we were in until needing to pay for something. Annoyingly, we paid 10CHF for two cold drinks from a shop in Switzerland when, 100m down the road, we could have stopped in a German café and paid half the price. Bloody maps. Perhaps GPS would have been more reliable after all. At 5.30pm it was 34°C, which meant that during the day we must have been cycling in temperatures around the 40°C mark. No wonder we had been hot and bothered.

We were entertained by a thunderstorm for the entire night on our first German campsite. I say entertained because I enjoy watching storms. The lightning was spectacular and we spent a fascinated hour or so watching it from under a convenient shelter next to the fast-flowing river. Once inside the tent, the noise from the thunder and rain was phenomenal and all I could think was that our lovely riverside pitch would become flooded and we would most likely be swept down along the mighty Rhine, never to be seen again. And so I spent a sleepless night, accompanied by the noise of thunder, rain and Iain's snoring because I rejected wearing my earplugs in case I missed the sound of a rising river, whatever sound that makes!

The storm seemed to do little to clear the air, as it remained hot and humid. Setting off the following day after little sleep seemed harder than usual, although we had by now got it down to just under an hour, including showers. The route now became increasingly hilly and more busy, with hundreds of leisure cyclists. We were accompanied by some who informed us it was a bank holiday. Somehow we were further along the route than we thought. When we stumbled upon the Rhine Falls, the place was packed, with thousands of tourists, tourist train, tourist boats, hundreds of cars, ice-cream sellers, hot-dog sellers and cafés. Even the obvious over-commercialisation of the area somehow couldn't overshadow the impressive sight and power of the falls themselves. They are the largest natural falls in Europe measuring 150m wide (450ft) and 23m high (75ft), with a phenomenal amount of water gushing through it. Despite us being on land a fair distance away, it made such an incredible racket that we could hardly hear each other speak. The killer hill on the way up and out of the place was an absolute bitch and a fitting Swiss finale.

Killer hills reminded us of our first ever encounter of Switzerland. After leaving the ambulance service, with two young children in tow, we took jobs in the Portes du Soleil ski area on the French–Swiss border. We had more than the necessary medical qualifications for the post, which basically involved looking after international schoolchildren based at a ski hotel. We, perhaps unintentionally, overstated our skiing ability. We had all returned from a one-week ski holiday in Andorra and now stupidly considered ourselves intermediate skiers. I don't consider my only other prior experience of skiing as a kid, which was the grand total of two days before ending up on crutches, to add any credence. Anyway, excited at arriving in our new surroundings (now feeling like confident intermediates), we took the kids (then 4 and 6) up to explore the local ski area. Going up went well and we tackled a couple of nice easy blue runs; we were in heaven. We could not quite believe how lucky we were to be swapping the intensity, responsibility and complications of both working on emergency ambulances and somehow juggling shift work and looking after two children for being paid to ski in a beautiful winter wonderland and live in a penthouse apartment (albeit decorated like a 1960s porn-star palace, complete with padded wallpaper and a jet-wash and blow-dry toilet!). Suddenly we were faced by what we could only describe as a terrifying drop over the abyss. Not only were we supposed to ski down it, but somehow we had to get two kids safely down there too. Shit!

After much deliberating and dilly-dallying at the top, constantly passed by a stream of competent skiers, many of whom took off and actively launched themselves over the edge, we decided upon the best (read no idea) route to take. Iain led, followed by the kids, and I went last in order to help if the kids fell over. Within seconds we were all on the floor. We got up and tried again. We all fell over again. It was carnage with us spread all over the slope. The kids decided sliding down on their bums was easier, and we tried joining them but gained speed at an alarming rate and shouted for them to try and stop as we tried desperately to dig anything, body part, pole or ski, into the snow. Then luckily another member of staff from our hotel appeared. With many years' skiing experience, he had a good, justified, laugh at our expense and then helped us by first skiing with our daughter between his skis, then whizzing up a lift and skiing back to us (in about one tenth of the time it took us to get there) and doing the same for our son, and then guiding us down too. I lost count of the number of times we fell on that first ever run back to the village, mostly because we were petrified at being flung off the edge of the narrow path and down the steep mountainside. We immediately signed up for some more lessons and, luckily, by the time we were needed for work and being towed behind the medic Ski-Doo, no one was any the wiser. And as for the kids, they ended up being amongst the packs of junior ski team terrors overtaking the rest of us on the slopes by jumping over our heads.

Chapter 15
Contrasts of Germany

We were aiming to spend the night on a campsite on the shores of Lake Zellersee (just prior to Lake Constance). There were several sites marked on the map, and with it being an obvious tourist area, we had higher than usual hopes of being successful. We rejected the first one we encountered as it was remote and we wanted to be nearer to a village (to have somewhere to look around on our day off). I feel it important to point out that there was no convenient, purpose-built flat route around the lake, it was road riding and up and down a series of quite serious hills. By now our cycling had improved to the point where on hills we were the bikes doing the overtaking, and it felt good. The next campsite, fairly close to the next village, was rejected as it was a bit shabby. Perhaps, we thought, we would strike third time lucky, some 10km away. As we approached potential number three, we could hear it was going to be no oasis! It would appear that a mini-Glastonbury festival was being held on site, and for some considerable distance around, the land was filled with vans, caravans, tents, loudspeaker music, acoustic music, chanting music, and more than the average number of dreadlocks per head of population. Although crowded, there was a nice, relaxed and calm atmosphere. Call us fussy if you like, but we just didn't fancy sharing toilet and shower facilities with so many, and it wasn't as if we weren't used to pressing on anyway. About 5pm, and off we continued up, up and up again this time.

Just outside the next village, in a magnificent pine forest, we passed several large groups of young men. Most groups were pulling a large trolley which was full of beer and was blaring out (mostly) rubbish German rap music at full volume. In the main, they were sozzled but seemed happy and friendly. Whilst I was struggling up one particularly steep section a few of them were a bit too friendly and thought it would be funny to stand in my way, whilst blowing kisses, and to jump out of the way at the last minute. The trouble was that drunk people rarely possess adequate motor skills or the co-ordination required to accomplish what they are intending. One of the idiots stayed in the way, and in frustration at having to slow down on the hill, I swore at him. I possess no German language skills whatsoever, and him being sworn at in English was apparently amusing to the rest of the group, who then all repeated my blaspheming in unison. He then tried to kiss me, which I found, at the very least, unpleasant, and as he was legless and stinking of alcohol, the amorous advance could best be described as repulsive. Instinctively, I kicked out and connected quite hard with his shin. How I remained upright I will never know. I powered off up the hill to the sound of his friends cheering and laughing, at me or him I'm not sure, and I wasn't going back to find out. Just for a change, Iain missed the whole episode. After Le Van Man incident, it was probably for the best as this one had a back-up crew of at least ten!

When we later told our German cyclist friends that I had encountered this incident, they were horrified. Here follows their own interpretation of what that day represents to some Germans. *"Once a year there is an event called Mannertag/Herrentag/Vatertag (Men's day) where rather than fathers or men spending time with and valuing their families, they are encouraged (in some areas) to celebrate their freedom from parental, or any other for that matter, responsibilities. Towing of a wagon full of beer and other alcohol before consuming it and becoming absolutely blind drunk is the favoured way to celebrate. It is quite frankly a ridiculous excuse for some men to behave like idiots and have a sauftag (drinking day). We are really sorry you experienced this."* Obviously, I hold them totally responsible for the whole of their nation's behaviour.

Finally, we stopped for the night on a little caravan park in the village of Iznang, where we pitched by the lake's edge and enjoyed a relaxing early evening looking at the boats, sunset and beautiful scenery. It then started to rain, so we went to the local pizzeria for shelter. It was a small strange caravan park, mostly occupied by caravan owners for the entire summer period. It had only four toilets and showers for the whole site, and the caravans did not have plumbing or their own facilities. We had to pay 50 cents to use the shower in addition to a rather expensive pitch fee, but it was nice and quiet, so we opted to have our rest day there. Annoyingly, the following day it was still raining and, as it seemed a bit of a waste spending all day in the tent, we took the ferry across the lake to Raadstat, in which it would appear the concept of public wi-fi has not yet been invented and is definitely not wanted. It was a miserable day really. We got soaking wet, there wasn't really much to see of any interest, and this always seemed a waste of a precious day out of the saddle.

The following morning we once again caught the ferry across to Raadstat, this time with our bikes and in the sunshine, an altogether more pleasurable experience. On the ferry journey we were accompanied by a family of cyclists (two adults, two primary-aged kids). Most of them were dressed appropriately for leisure cycling, i.e. casual clothes and cycle helmets, but the dad seemed to be taking it all a bit too seriously. He had the top-of-the-range mountain bike, padded elbows, knees, shorts, Lycra sports top, neck scarf, gloves, backpack, water Camelbak, water bottles, phone holder and more GPS gadgets than a spaceship, all the gear. None of them smiled or acknowledged us. The route signage in Germany was different from what we had previously encountered. The EuroVelo 6 signs completely disappeared and the ones which replaced them were infuriating. We would see signs to the same village or town in two or more different directions. It eventually became apparent to us that they were local scenic circuits. By the time we had worked it out, we had cycled 52km to cover a distance of just 35km. On the upside, it gave us the opportunity to twice overtake "all the gear" man on his leisurely scenic journey.

Unsurprisingly, he didn't look impressed on either occasion.

The previous evening's pizza, or perhaps the beer, left Iain suffering with a dodgy stomach most of the night and hot sweats for most of the following day. It was probably not the best day, therefore, to be cycling entirely uphill all day. Don't forget we chose this route as it is described as flat (remember the quote from the EuroVelo website?) *"EuroVelo 6, from the Atlantic to the Black Sea, is one of our most popular routes and it's little wonder why: coasts, rivers, castles and a nice flat topography make it every cycle tourists' dream journey"*. A nice flat topography – are they mad? I beg to differ. Whoever wrote it most certainly had not completed this section, which was six bloody hours entirely uphill. We even passed ski lifts and communication towers, in case they needed further clues. Thank goodness it wasn't near the beginning of our trip, as I'm sure we could not have made it and would have given up. I was amazed and impressed that Iain with his gippy tummy made it. Thankfully, it was a series of hills with bends, through pine forests, and each time we would aim for a bend, hoping and praying we would finally have reached the top of the hill. Of course, each time we were disappointed, but at least we couldn't see the full extent of what we were expected to climb all at once.

We were hoping to be rewarded by an amazing downhill section, but sadly it was unimpressive, especially when compared to the amount of effort put in to get to the top.

We gently rolled down no more than about 5km into the town of Tuttlingen. The hills surrounding the town are the source of the River Danube. We would be following this river now all the way to the Black Sea, but first we had a campsite to find. We were directed to the park where the campsite was apparently located. The park was impressive with sports pitches, skate park, cafés, picnic areas, exercise facilities, nature areas and the infant River Danube running through it. We saw it all at least twice. It was full of people enjoying a day of leisure. Still unable to find the campsite and now on our third or fourth ride past a group of people of (probably) Moroccan origin, we stopped to speak to them as we could hear them speaking French. They directed us to the local swimming pool where we could collect the campsite keys. They also showed us the campsite, which was a tiny square of hedged-in grass between the railway line, works yard and the football teams' changing room. According to the sign it was *"the most wonderful facility offered to travellers who visit Tuttlingen"*. Blimey, we joked, wonder what the least wonderful facilities are like. At the swimming pool we were given a key (after leaving a 20 euro deposit) to the football team shower block. With no cubicles, no shower curtains or designated male and female areas but twenty clean showers to choose from, we were rather pleased that no one else had booked to stay at this most wonderful facility, and I was particularly pleased that the football team wasn't playing that day! It was no big surprise that we were woken just before 6am by both trains and workmen.

The Germans could probably learn a thing or two from the French about what constitutes a good campsite.

Due to our early-morning rude awakening, we could at least set off at a reasonable time for a change. It was annoying to discover the swimming pool didn't open until 9am and we had to wait to get our key deposit back. As usual, when getting out of town, both the map and the signage were about as useful as chocolate teapots and we started the day off just a little bit grumpy.

We were then cheered up considerably as we entered the most beautiful and abundant areas of wildflower meadows that either of us have ever seen. Every shade of every colour seemed to be represented amongst the long grass. It was stunning. We cycled through mile upon mile of meadows accompanying the meandering of the young River Danube (Donau in German) through the impressive limestone valley of the Obere Donau National Park. With castles and buildings perched high up on the top of impressive limestone cliffs, the smell of fresh flowers and grass wafting towards us in the light breeze, and bright green trees all in full glorious sunshine, we both agreed that this experience was the most pleasurable cycling day of the entire trip. Perhaps we were going to enjoy our German experience after all.

Chapter 16
Bogey men

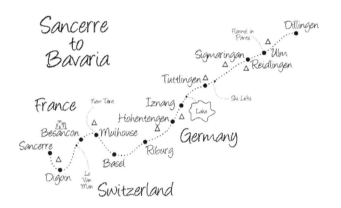

Sancerre to Bavaria

Dillingen

Flannel in Pants

Sigmaringan Ulm
Reidlingen

Tuttlingen

France   New Tent   Iznang   Lake   Ski Lifts

Hohentengen

Besançon Mulhouse   Germany

Sancerre   Riburg

Basel

Digoin   Le
Van
Man   Switzerland

There seems to be no way of buttering or jazzing it up, we found Bavarian Germany dull. Yes, every village or town that we passed through was jam-packed with excessively huge, elaborate-fronted buildings painted in cute pastel colours and looking like something that would have been at home on the front of a chocolate box; there's no denying the countryside and towns were beautiful. Everywhere, houses, gardens, villages and towns were neat, tidy and perfect. On several occasions we saw people with small road-sweeping machines (the size of a push lawnmower) sweeping the area of pavement outside their perfectly swept and manicured driveways, such was the level of attention to detail. It was so perfect that, for some reason, it unnerved me. It probably sounds ridiculous, but I wrote in my diary of feeling almost like there was some type of sinister presence. It reminded me of something that at first I couldn't quite place.

So, when we came across a landslide on the riverside path between Sigmaringen and Reidlingen, we were oddly pleased, with both the lack of order and the challenge. Initially we were warned of the potential hazard by a large barrier and a "Route Closed" sign. We ignored it, moved the barrier and continued. The alternative route was four times longer and no doubt it wouldn't be flat. When we saw a cyclist coming from the other direction, we figured it couldn't be closed after all. Fully laden and covered in mud, he was the first touring cyclist we had seen in a long time. We had a good chat and we learned that he had already completed the route to the Black Sea and was now on his way to Norway. When we asked if we could get through, he said, "Yes, it's muddy and a bit dangerous, and you'll have to unload and portage in sections, but it's still much easier than the alternative route which is over a huge hill."

Talking to the other touring cyclist made us realise what it was that we were finding difficult. He was the first person who had been happy to talk to us in days. All the way through France and Switzerland fellow cyclists were friendly and at the very least would smile and wave hello. Here in Bavaria we noticed that most cyclists didn't respond at all or reply to our waves with greetings of *guten Tag*, *Morgen* or even a friendly nod. If we did get a reaction, it would be to actually turn or look away from us. Were they shy or rude? We couldn't work it out. The reasonably priced campsites of France, with leisure facilities and staff or owners who would be interested in our journey, were replaced by extortionately overpriced sites (at least three times the cost) where, more often than not, we then had to pay extra for showers which were often dirty with no curtains, and where internet access was mostly not possible or would also cost extra. We got the distinct impression that Bavarians believe campsites are only frequented by inferior people who can't afford a proper holiday and who therefore should not expect any more than the bare minimum standards. Whereas travelling by bike seems to appeal to the nature of freedom valued so dearly by the French, it seemed to be inconceivable to the Bavarians that respectable people would choose to camp and cycle carrying all of their belongings for pleasure. Why would we do that when we could go by car? It would surely be more efficient and, well, tidy.

A large section of the cliff had fallen into the river and taken about a 10m (30ft) section of path with it. It was a wet, clay-mud mess. It did have a small indent of a newly formed path made by people like the aforementioned cyclist, which helped. I wouldn't have liked to have been the first across; it was treacherous and one wrong footing would have us sliding several metres down into the freezing-cold river below. We unloaded our bags from the bikes and proceeded to carry what we could manage in our arms across to the other side, slipping and sliding as we went. After repeating this several times, and with the bags safely across, we returned for the bikes. This was even more difficult. The track (if you could even call it that) was extremely narrow and all Solo and Polo wanted to do was obey gravity and pull us down with them.

As we packed up after negotiating the landslide, it started to rain. At least it's only drizzle, we thought. A couple of hours later we were soaked. And just as we thought it couldn't get any worse, it did. As we cycled along an exposed ridge between Reidlingen and Ulm, the freezing-cold wind picked up and simultaneously almost blew us off the bikes whilst chucking buckets of ice-cold torrential rain at us. The ridge, the wind and the rain continued for what seemed like an eternity. There were no parts of exposed skin that weren't being seriously stung by the rain. And then, once again when we thought it couldn't possibly get any worse, it turned to hail! There was nowhere to shelter; we just had to keep going. It was truly miserable. Eventually, we did spot a barn with an overhanging roof to shelter under, but it was far too late. We were already soaked through to what felt like the bone, and we were probably in danger of hypothermia. Our lips were definitely blue and our teeth chattering like wind-up comedy teeth. Fortified and uplifted by the surprise discovery of rum in a chocolate bar that we had thought was just plain old fruit and nut, we set off again, deciding it was warmer to keep going than to stand still. We became just a little bit addicted to this chocolate.

Thankfully, the town we passed through after a couple of hours' freezing cold and wet cycling possessed a very welcome sight in the form of a café. We entered the café still freezing cold and more than just a bit wet. Luckily, they had coat hangers above a radiator to hang our wet-on-the-inside coats on. They instantly deposited large pools of water on the floor. We each visited the toilets, hoping for an air hand dryer more than anything else, but we were disappointed to find just a pile of neatly folded small white hand towels. I had taken a change of bra and T-shirt into the loo and I dried myself off, as best as I could with a flannel! Neither of us had spare dry cycling shorts to change into. We sat ourselves at one end of a cushioned bench seat and ordered soup. It was delicious and just what we needed. We ordered more and moved along the bench onto a dry spot. It was going to be some time before we dried our bottoms off using this method! Iain had decided that the hand towels were the perfect size for stuffing into his cycle shorts to perform both a warming and drying role, and I almost choked on my soup with laughter as he told me he still had a flannel in his pants, and he felt he was completely justified as he considered the situation to be a state of emergency. After another couple of hot drinks, cake, more flannel changing (in the toilet, I hasten to add) and much shuffling along to the next dry portion of cushioned bench, we paid up and pushed off. My apologies to the café owners and staff. And sorry, Bavarians, perhaps you are right and camping cyclists are indeed messy undesirable types.

Maybe it was the cold, rain, hail, carrying the luggage over the landslide or just all the hill cycling, but Iain developed a bad neck and was unable to turn his head to the right. We bought Tiger Balm and replaced the Diclofenac used during the coccyx crisis. Luckily, being abroad, we mostly needed to look left, so, although painful, it wasn't going to be a dangerous affliction.

Before we got there, we were looking forward to Germany. The German family we had met on the tour in France had been fantastic people and were likely to become long-term friends. We were also looking forward to trying the famous sausages and visiting a country we had no previous experience of. We came to the conclusion that once you have tasted one exceedingly over-processed sausage with no clue as to which type of animal it contains, you've tasted them all. Give me a proper British butcher's sausage any day. We soon became sick of sausages and the lack of choice of unprocessed meat, but did come across a few amazing farmers' fruit and vegetable markets. We also met a Swiss cyclist, who, having travelled through Germany before, said, *"I am this time prepared and bring my own ham"* as he pulled out a previously whole, but now partially eaten, leg from his rear pannier!

As we crossed Bavaria, the general state of shower and toilet facilities seemed to deteriorate, especially in the men's blocks. It would appear that whereas most women would ensure the toilet is clean after use – using the handily supplied brush for this purpose, most men do not; many don't even bother to flush. Most women do not spend half an hour each morning coughing up phlegm and spitting it out, depositing it in and around sinks and shower cubicles for other people to tread in, lean on or generally experience. Most women don't even bother with the coughing stage, let alone the disgusting leave it for someone else to clean up stage. I thought the occasional unflushed toilet, plugholes full of matted hair or pubes on the wall were bad enough, and as a rule, these were the worst traits of just some of the female blocks. When a site was empty or quiet, I would stand guard so that Iain could use the female facilities. He was understandably becoming more and more disgusted, annoyed and weary of the standards left by his fellow man, often feeling dirtier on exit than entrance. In order to cope, he bought himself a pair of designated shower shoes and anti-bacterial wipes for when sneakily using the female facilities was not an option. This wasn't just a case of us being fussy. Iain has OCD, and coping with this was probably more of a challenge to him than the actual cycling was. Because he does have incredibly high standards, at first I (perhaps) didn't really appreciate how bad things were in the men's block. I don't have OCD so I did a little inspection for myself; from what I saw and heard of the phlegm coughing and shit-smeared pans, I would never want to experience it again. It was most disgusting.

Eventually, being surrounded by unfriendly people, a lack of decent food and incredibly low hygiene standards really got to us and began to really affect our morale. At this point we felt and discussed in detail that it was most probable that all of these things were just going to get worse the further east we headed. I got the distinct impression that Iain would rather be heading to Italy. If I wasn't so stubborn and felt we had a goal to achieve, I would probably have decided to head to Italy too. It would definitely be a lot more pleasant and we both wanted to go there anyway. There was also the question of the charity we were raising money for and all of the Nordic Walkers back home expecting us to reach the Black Sea.

One lunchtime we passed through a town called Donauwörth. It possessed the usual massive but beautiful pastel-coloured buildings, but instead of having the usual deserted and spooky atmosphere, it was full of families enjoying a bank-holiday festival. This was when it struck us that it was a distinct lack of children we had subconsciously noticed in other towns and villages we had passed through, and what it reminded us of was the setting of the film *Chitty Chitty Bang Bang*. Anyway, it was a nice change to experience some energy and joy, so we stopped for lunch and treated ourselves to some stunning kirsch and cherry ice cream before joking that we ought to rush off in order to stay one step ahead of the child snatchers.

Chapter 17
Lederhosen

We were overjoyed when we stumbled upon a campsite with a brand-new state-of-the-art shower and facilities block larger than the terminal building at Bournemouth Airport. We didn't even mind too much that it cost us over 35 euros to camp there for the night or that it had no internet. It was clean, and that was all that mattered after our recent encounters. With only about twenty caravans on site and a small patch of grass suitable for ten campers at the most, we wondered why such a large building was necessary, but again, were past caring really. It was clean, wonderfully warm and if it hadn't been for the awful piped music (it really was like an airport), we would have considered bedding down on the benches in the corridor if we thought we could have got away with it.

The campsite owner told us he had no internet, and, no, there was no internet in the town. They do not need it, he explained. We could hear loudspeakers and wandered into town anyway, where it appeared that there was some type of fair taking place. We first walked through a cheap, tacky and tatty clothing market, where most of the items would have been rejected by a UK or French market stall holder, which is saying something. There were a couple of better stalls amongst them and also a large number of stalls selling lederhosen. These were clearly of good quality and extremely expensive. Most of the people in town and in the market were wearing traditional Bavarian lederhosen or dresses, which was nice to see. We wandered into the fair, which was more or less exactly the same as it would be in the UK: bright lights, excessively loud competing music coming from each ride, screams of excitement as the rides tumbled back to earth at tremendous speeds, men pushing the girls around on the Waltzer, hot dogs and candy floss. At the far end, and taking up even more space than the fairground itself, were the beer tents and endless rows of trestle tables filled with lederhosen-clad beer-swilling people having a good time. We clearly weren't local dressed in our casual camping clothes, and despite our best efforts to engage with or talk to someone, anyone, we were ignored. We finished our half pints, watched a man making cigars by hand, bought some socks and left disappointed.

We were now really keen to leave Germany but had become worried by reports that the Austrian campsites could be even more expensive. At the German rate of 35 euros per night, we were already forking out a ridiculous amount, more than 1,000 euros per month. You could seriously rent a real house for less. We considered wild camping in Germany to keep costs down. It would also have probably been cleaner, but we were advised it was illegal and we didn't want the risk of being moved on or arrested to add to our misery.

For our final section of cycling in Germany we were once again accompanied by incredibly stunning scenery, which went some way to lifting our spirits. It was a bank holiday, and the route was almost as busy as a motorway as we followed it alongside the Danube. We entered the Danube

Gorge and where the path discontinued at the site of a monastery, we loaded our bikes onto a ferry for a 20-minute section. Sitting on the roof, we passed through the absolutely stunning gorge, drinking hot chocolate and appreciating every minute of movement without having to pedal.

Our final German campsite cost 28 euros per night, plus it had ridiculous 50-cent slots for a shower. I say ridiculous because the slot was located outside the cubicle and the only-just-warm water stream only lasted long enough to get wet and get shampoo on, at high speed, but not long enough to get aforementioned shampoo rinsed off again. This meant stepping out of the shower dripping wet, covered in soap and naked, finding another coin, opening the door, walking around the corner to put another coin in (still naked, so as not to get only towel soapy) and then racing back in to rinse off, the cubicle floor now being soaking wet. Grrr! They also wanted another 5 euros for the privilege of using the internet. We went without – money-grabbing buggers.

As we were eating our pre-dinner crisps and having a glass of wine, a French bike-touring couple turned up and were shown where they could pitch by a member of staff. They decided on a pitch opposite to us. A few minutes later, the German campsite owner arrived in his van, screeched to a halt and proceeded to scream and shout abuse at them, with much arm waving and gesticulation. Apparently, they had pitched in a caravan spot and were not allowed to be where they were. His effort at their relocation was a gross over-reaction and certainly contained zero customer-service qualities. Annoyingly for them, it was just starting to rain. Had they been allowed to stay where they were, they would have got away without any inconvenience. Even moving a few feet meant repacking bedding into the panniers to prevent it getting wet. We invited them to pitch next to us, gave them a hand and, over a glass of wine, we all agreed that the short German guy might just have anger issues and perhaps modelled himself on a certain historical German figure and was definitely an arsehole. No one else arrived or used the vacated pitch, making it seem all the more ridiculous.

We all had dinner in the restaurant (the room) behind the campsite bar. We had asparagus soup (passable) followed by what the French couple couldn't even begin to comprehend and what we would describe as being worse than the worst type of school canteen dinner either of us had ever experienced. Frozen schnitzel (not quite even warm) and a pile of cream coloured mush – was it potato, pasta or something else, we debated and could not come to a decision – and a pile of soggy green stuff, which was once allegedly asparagus. It was possibly the worst meal we have ever had the privilege to pay for. Hospital food would have been preferable.

After visiting the ladies' loo I walked through the bar and was surprised to find Iain and the French couple sitting around a table with a group of Bavarians in traditional costume complete with two accordions. Apparently, they were waiting for me to arrive so we could all join them in singing a well-known traditional Bavarian song. We were handed a song sheet (all Greek to me) and were shown where we were expected to join in with the yodelling parts! Luckily, they were all incredibly drunk and thought we were amazing. They then handed Iain one of the accordions and he made a series of noises which hurt my ears but strangely impressed them. We were then toasted as being honorary Bavarians and they kept repeating Iain's (clearly amusing to them) version of a Bavarian toast. We left before it became any more messy and before I punched the lecherous old man sat next to me, who kept trying to put his hand on my thigh. These were the only smiling Bavarians we met.

The following morning it was peeing with rain and we discovered an indoor kitchen where, if you put 50 cents into the slot you could use an electric hob for about 90 seconds. We and the French couple decided to take our own stoves to the kitchen and use them there – much more sensible. Well, it was all sensible and going well until the French guy, proudly showing us his own hand-made and personally fashioned from a Coke can Trangia-type burner, managed to knock it over, spilling lighted methylated spirits all over the work surfaces and electric hobs and setting fire to the kitchen. Oops! After hastily patting out the fire and a quick wipe over, we all decided it was probably time to leave.

Chapter 18
Reaching Bratislava

When we crossed into Austria we had been on our bikes for two months. We had become fed up with the generally unfriendly attitude of the Germans that we had encountered and were also annoyed that at the end of May we were still experiencing pretty shit weather. We were hoping that things would improve for our Austrian section. They didn't! The cycling part was now proving to be the easier part of the challenge.

We were both feeling the strain. An excerpt from my diary has a rare fit of capital letters and says *"ABSOLUTELY FED UP WITH SEEING BLOODY MISERABLE PEOPLE – REALLY GETTING TO ME AND IAIN."* We were being a bit cross and snappy with each other too, which was unlike us, and it was just the wonderful news we needed when we found out that our son Aaron and his girlfriend Abbie were going to fly out and meet us in Vienna in three days' time. Vienna was 226km away. We had better get a wriggle on and stop moping about.

We covered the 106km section between Linz and Melk in just one day. With our own outward and inward smiles restored, we still received nothing but seriousness and sternness in return. Maybe, we wondered, their faces would crack if they smiled. Perhaps they just thought we were crazy? With campsites indeed proving more expensive than in Germany, we were pleased to be speeding through and not stopping too often. There were now no shower curtains for privacy and there was a change in the shape of toilet pan; they now had a specially

142

designed poo-catching shelf for self-analysis and worm-checking purposes.

We passed through an area where flooding had been an obvious hazard for hundreds of years but the frequency and severity of these was perhaps becoming more of an issue. The bike path was often on the top of newly erected high dykes formed to encircle and protect entire villages. We cycled through new, open massive high flood gates which would be closed in the event of a flood warning, and more often than not they had a marker indicating the date and the height of the last floodwaters. We wondered whether making the gate only a few centimetres higher than the last flood was high enough! On one campsite the accompanying bar had marked the flood levels from the previous couple of centuries in decorative iron on the side of its wall. Often the water had risen higher than the second floor windows. We took a walk into town from the campsite one evening. Once again, everything was perfectly painted, perfectly decorated and perfectly arranged, with nothing out of place. Feeling a little bit mischievous, I moved a plant pot, just a couple of centimetres out of place. Iain laughed and moved a chair, just a little bit. By the time we had walked home, we were in hysterics. Every pot and bench had been moved; some now even faced the opposite way, some had been moved across to the other side of the road, and one was even balanced on its end! And we hadn't even had a drink.

In Zwentendorf we had an awful night on a campsite in a sports field. The toilet block and adjacent car park were both evidently frequented all night by young people and their cars too in skidding-to-very-loud-rap-music competitions. Thankfully, the competitors didn't use the ladies'! Their music, well, hideous loud rap noise, continued until the early hours. We were pleased to leave but were not what you could describe as well rested. I decided to play some music of our own whilst packing up that day. An emotional song caught us out and brought us both to tears. Although we knew we would be seeing at least one of our kids the next day, we had still missed them both, and I think it showed how low we were feeling and how difficult we were finding being removed from our usual more regular family contact.

In order to cheer myself up, I decided to place my iPod and miniature speaker into my handlebar bag and to play loud up-beat music for the last leg into Vienna. It worked wonders. Singing along to Michael Jackson or whichever random song played as it jumped and changed if I went over particularly bumpy section made me feel much happier. We cycled together and sang at the top of our voices to the Queen hit "Bicycle" and Mark Ronson's "The Bike Song". We were enjoying ourselves again. We were looked at with disapproval. It was almost as if we were breaking the law, and still no one smiled. Wish we had thought of it sooner.

We reached Vienna and easily found our way around to our hotel using the highly impressive and many designated cycle lanes. With the seemingly free use of the underground system (well no one else seemed to be paying either!), we had an amazing couple of days with Aaron and Abbie, cramming in as many tourist sites as humanly possible. We timed it well and all the rose gardens were in full bloom and the sun was shining. We even spotted a man with a reindeer head busking with an accordion. It was full-on. Our feet ached and it wasn't a rest, but it was definitely a welcome change to our schedule. After discovering no obvious eating districts in Vienna, and keen to avoid any more schnitzel, we ate in a different Italian restaurant each night. After dinner one evening, we wandered around looking for a bar outside in which to have a digestif and a coffee. We were told by a restaurant that we could drink coffee but only inside as it was after 11pm. It was a law to prevent disturbance, but with people clearly still eating outside, it seemed ridiculous.

Literally bathing in and enjoying the luxury of our hotel room, with our own clean bathroom, we didn't depart until almost 10.30am. Iain then decided he needed coffee and so we stopped as soon as we crossed onto the north side of the Danube, a mere 20 minutes later. This was turning out to be much like one of Iain's ski days. He then spotted a barber shop and decided to get his hair cut properly. A good plan, seeing as up until this point, I had been cutting it with clippers. I have no experience or talent for cutting hair, and although I had been given one demonstration by his regular barber prior to leaving, I was remarkably rubbish at it, and on my first attempt had managed to include a couple of bald patches. I ordered another coffee and waited patiently for the professional to put right my handiwork. Ten minutes short of an hour, he finally emerged and did look much better for it. Hopefully, I would now be relieved of all hairdressing duties.

Now almost midday, we finally set off along the banks of the Danube in an easterly direction. The first couple of miles or so appeared to be designated nudist bathing areas. Either that or all Austrians sunbathe naked. Quite a few seemed to be exhibitionists and on seeing us approach, would jump up, stretch, do exercises, run alongside us or leap across the path in front of us. There were not many other dressed people about; they could have so easily waited for us to pass and chosen a spectator-free moment. When taking the opportunity to fill up our water bottles at a drinking-water tap, there was an apparent and sudden need for a whole group of naked people to form a queue next to the waist-height taps, which meant we were bent over with our heads inconveniently placed at roughly sausage and two veg level! This got us wondering what the group noun for a group of naked people might be, and we decided that if there wasn't one already, "wibble", "wobble" or "nobble" might be good candidates. We passed by an outside café just as a dressed family were joined at their table by a nude gentleman. There were plenty of empty tables to choose from. We decided on this occasion not to stop.

The route was straight, mainly flat and with a good surface. We first passed huge petroleum-processing plants and then got onto tree-lined paths. Irritatingly, the trees were too far away from the path to offer any shade from the day's fiercely hot sun, but they were also tall and thick enough to block out any views of the river. As the temperature got hotter and hotter, we both got a bit cross and had a stupid argument, about what I fail to recall, and after which I spent a couple of hours cycling in tears.

Then in the distance we could see hundreds of ugly, identical communist-style flats on a hillside, a complete contrast to anything we had seen so far. Now we really were entering previously unexperienced territory, and for the first time it felt more like a real expedition than a holiday. As we crossed over the Slovakian border, our row was soon forgotten after a hug, and we realised our tetchiness probably had something to do with knowing we wouldn't be seeing our kids for at least another couple of months.

Before setting off I had made a collection of small laminated cards with the essentials of each language on them. Hello, bike, campsite, hospital, bread, shop, water, etc. Our budget wasn't intended to stretch to hotels, so this wasn't a featured word. Armed with the new word for hello in Slovakian, we started to greet people with a friendly *"ahoy"* (not making it up!) and were rewarded once again (thank goodness!) with smiles and returned greetings. We were overjoyed. We had really had enough of misery and being made to feel unwelcome. We continued along the EuroVelo 6, passing the old fortifications (now a museum – which annoyingly was closed and we didn't have time to return) built to defend the old communist Czechoslovakia against Austria. As there were no campsites in the capital city of Bratislava, on the internet in Austria we had booked ourselves a hotel for the grand sum of 25 euros including breakfast. Armed with a picture (in our heads) of the river view and surrounding buildings, we entered the city and looked for the riverside Botel Veronica. Bratislava was a beautiful city and we were keen to have a proper look around the following day. That day, however, we just wanted to find our hotel. After several turns around the same riverside area, we couldn't find it. We asked and were directed to another part of town that we hadn't yet seen, so were hopeful, but it was wrong. We were guided back towards the river by a fellow cyclist who ran the local cycling café and had come across Crazy Harry and Johnny a few days ago. A botel, she explained, was not the Slovakian word for hotel (as we had assumed), it was an actual boat–hotel hybrid. The Americans had thought the same, so at least we weren't the only ignorant idiots.

We pushed Solo and Polo on board and, after locking them up safely in the foyer, we carted our many panniers down two flights of stairs to our room. Although the bathroom was too small to sit on the toilet without hitting your knees on the wall, it was at least clean and en suite, and for that we were incredibly grateful. The bed was big and had real sheets too. Our camping gear enjoyed a night off duty and we headed out for dinner. We knew nothing about Slovakian cuisine and expected our experience to probably be similar or worse than in Austria. We were blown away and had a magnificently huge plate of pork ribs, from pigs raised in the mountains of Slovakia. They were outstanding and after a month of processed rubbish, we were incredibly impressed that they were both real meat and the restaurant appeared to even care about their provenance. We devoured every scrap of meat off every bone like starving vultures.

Chapter 19
A day of two halves

We loved Bratislava, a compact, friendly city the perfect size for a weekend break. We only had a day to look around but I think we managed to see the main sites and were lucky to stumble upon a live band playing in the main square after our meal out. The city was full of quirky and fun statues installed originally to help rid the city of the greyness of the communist era. With abundant cafés, there were plenty of places to sit around, people watch and sample some of the local cake, a type of pastry filled with poppy-seed paste and cherries, not overly sweet but definitely delicious.

We had difficulty finding our way out of Bratislava. You'd think that with a major river running right through the centre, you would just need to follow it in an easterly direction. It couldn't be that hard, could it? Firstly, the road, which did run along the south side of the river, and would have been the easiest route to find or follow, was completely closed, dug up and being moved. So we had to cross over one bridge and work our way along the north side to another bridge. The trouble was, there were no signs, our map was completely wrong (just for a change) and many of the roads on the north side were also being dug up and moved to line up with a new bridge from the opposite side. In essence, we just had to keep cycling roughly towards the old bridge but kept being herded towards the new bridge, which was not yet completed. On one of our dead-end routes we ended up down a narrow path and there at the end was something like a scene from the movies: several burly suited men, shaven headed, non-smiling, thickset jawlines, with arms crossed and no doubt a gun or two each, were standing menacingly in a circle around a fire. Shit! we thought and very quickly turned round and cycled back to where we had come from. Once again I was grateful for my improved bike-handling skills.

Still not finding the bridge, we asked a fellow cyclist for help. She very kindly said she was heading that way, and if we wanted we could follow her. I think she was late for work or something because she set off at a breakneck speed and we had trouble keeping up with her. She led us through paths between blocks of flats, over a main road, under a main road, over a bridge, under a pass, along a narrow path within a strip of wasteland and then through more blocks of flats and finally onto the bridge. There was absolutely no way on this planet that we could have found our own way. Unless she was having a laugh and just fancied seeing a couple of fully laden tourers ride at full speed in unnecessary circles. We thanked her as she disappeared at top speed into the distance.

Now back alongside the Danube, we passed a boatyard full of huge rusting boats making eerie squeaking and groaning sounds, almost as if they were alive but only just so and uttering their dying words. We passed a few other cyclists and I happily greeted them with a loud and enthusiastic "hoopla!" All day I continued, and was impressed by the general friendliness, smiling, laughing and return greetings. It wasn't until later looking at my list for the word for shop when I realised I had completely made up the word "hoopla". The actual word for hello was "ahoy". Well, at least the crazy English woman had given everyone something to smile about.

Immediately on leaving the city we were in beautiful countryside. The cycle path was perfectly smooth tarmac. The weather was hot with a very slight and welcome tailwind. The river on our right widened and it was now more like cycling by the sea than a river, and it had, at last, become the Blue Danube. To our left we had a wide area of lush green grass, dotted with wild flowers, then a canal, and every now and again a quaint little village between the canal and the fields in the distance. This was by far the most perfect cycling weather conditions and surface combination that we had experienced to date. The tripometer registered my average speed as an impressive 28km/hr, and for some stretches Iain was effortlessly zooming along at 38km/hr. We were making progress and enjoying every minute of it.

We stopped for lunch on the shady terrace of a dilapidated football stadium. Although it was deserted, the loudspeakers were blaring out what sounded like a match commentary (given my recent linguistic failure I cannot confirm this was actually the case), but regardless of what it was, it was quite frankly a bit spooky, and when the water sprinklers suddenly switched themselves on I almost jumped out of my skin. Feeling pleased with our morning progress, we treated ourselves to a short and rare after-lunch nap and then set off again, both feeling well fed, happy, rested and looking forward to more in the same vein as the morning.

Shortly after lunch, the surface changed to shallow gravel, then shortly after that, to deep gravel. It was almost impossible to keep the fully laden bike upright, and had this been near the beginning of the trip, I would not have been able to. I was proud of the improvement in my bike-handling ability but we were both immensely frustrated that our perfect surface had been replaced by deep gravel. Instead of averaging 30km/hr or so, we were now covering perhaps 3km/hr, if that. In most places it was quicker and easier to walk. There was no way that this was a surface suitable for a long-distance touring bike route, and now with the fine gravel replaced in sections by large smooth moving stones, it was more like trying to cycle on Brighton beach, almost impossible.

As if this wasn't challenging enough, we were now encountering some allegedly bike-friendly barriers. These barriers reached across the track to prevent motorised traffic access but they had a U-shaped bend in the centre through which cyclists were supposed to be able to pass. Had either the bottom of the U been anywhere near the floor or the barrier not have been a good few inches thick, we might have been in with a chance! Perhaps placing one barrier every 100 metres or so could have been considered excessive enough, but placing four to six of them in close succession (3m/9ft apart) every 100m metres or so seemed ridiculous. On each barrier encounter we had to dismount and lift our bikes over or, on the rare occasions where the barrier was floor level, we attempted a kind of BMX-style jump where we pulled up on the handlebars to get the front wheel over the barrier and then, standing on the pedals, hope we were going fast enough for the rear wheel to follow, all whilst trying not to topple over sideways in the gravel and hitting our luggage (which only just fitted through) on the barriers. It didn't always work and we both came a cropper a couple of times.

We soon realised that there was no possible way that we were going to make our targeted campsite and it was a welcome bit of good luck to see a handwritten sign for a campsite just 200m away at the next junction off to a village. We eagerly cycled in the direction of the village and soon came across a man sitting on a bench in his front driveway with another home-made camping sign nailed to a post above his head. "Yes," he said. "Camping yes," whilst his dog went crazy at us from behind a fence. At this moment, a young lady appeared on a bike and stopped to say hello. Thankfully, she spoke English and we asked her to ask the gentleman where the camping was and what facilities he had. She spoke to him and then after he replied looked at us and said quickly, "You must go now. Smile and wave to the man and go that way. I will meet you at the vending machine." We did as we were told. "He is a crazy man. I don't think it is safe to stay there. He has no camping, no toilet even, and I am not even sure what he was saying some of the time." We thanked her, bought each of us a drink from the vending machine (weirdly situated in the middle of nowhere) and got out the map.

We were certainly not going to get to the campsite that day if we continued along the Brighton beach route, so instead opted to take the roads. The surfaces were indeed better, but the traffic was dismally dangerous. Neither cars nor trucks slowed or widened their path to overtake, so we felt it safest to cycle amongst the random road debris on the narrow strip of rough tarmac on the verge side of the white line. It was a scary and unpleasant experience and we were pleased when we turned off the main road and onto a more local route into Zlatna na Ostore. We were less pleased to discover the campsite had closed years ago and we had to get back onto Hell Highway for another 6km or so, only to discover yet again that there was no campsite.

Rather than search for the campsite in the following town, Iain called into a bar to ask directions. From the outside the bar looked like it might be bike friendly (a couple of bikes in the entrance hall), but he came out with a hideous description of a smoke-filled room, full of dirty, filthy, stinking men, some with their heads on the tables snoring and the others completely and utterly pissed but just about staying upright (it was about 5pm). No one was willing or able to offer any assistance. A passing taxi stopped and told us there was no longer "a camping" in this town, we needed to go on to the next one, it wasn't too far. People in cars, we learned, always seem to under-estimate both distance and the severity of hills. Several kilometres of uphill later, in busy and dangerous rush-hour traffic, we arrived in Komarno. It was almost 6.30pm and we had been in the saddle (mostly) since 9am and had covered over 100km. We stopped to ask people where the campsite was, and although they were friendly, it was clear that it wasn't in the immediate vicinity, and the directions to get to it were quite complicated. Eventually, a man on a bike decided it would be easier for us to follow him than for him to try and describe how to get there. What seemed like an eternity later, after passing right through the city and into a warren of paths through communist-style blocks of flats, we arrived at a football stadium. "This is camping," he said. We thanked him and offered him a drink. He wouldn't accept and said it was just his pleasure to help visitors. What a gentleman.

The receptionist gave us keys for the campsite gate, the shower block and the thermal spa (which closed at 8pm). With the discovery that none of the showers had curtains, we quickly hot-footed it over to the thermal spa, not really knowing what to expect but hoping it would at least be warm. It was incredible. For about 10 euros not only did we have a camping pitch but the use of three swimming pools and three different hot spring pools. We only had time to sample one of them for a 15-minute soak that evening, but after the day we had had, it was pure bliss. We planned to test out the others in the morning.

Chapter 20
Hungry in Hungary

That evening we met fellow tourers from France who were heading for Montenegro. Mateus and Fanny, a brother and sister, both doctors, he computer and she medical, they had toured before and usually travelled on a tandem, but as it was currently off the road they were on borrowed bikes for one last European tour before he headed off to live in America. During the mutual bike and luggage assessment, they tried, but couldn't really hide their surprise at the size of my bike. We shared an evening meal of processed sausages and the most plastic cheese I have ever encountered, but we all had a fantastic and sociable evening.

The four of us spent an hour in the thermal spa in the morning and we all ordered the delicious-looking chocolate-sauce-coated pancakes that we had spotted at the café. None of us expected them to be filled with cottage cheese flavoured with artificial lemon, which seemed to taste like what I would imagine washing-up liquid to be like. We also weren't expecting to see a woman of mature years and ample weight who was the spitting image of Gary Glitter, complete with jet-black bouffant hairstyle and full-on double black eyeliner lines across her face, lounging around in a sequinned bikini! After exchanging details (with the cyclists, not Gary), we headed off on our separate ways.

An hour or so later we were cycling over yet another bridge, this time into Hungary. Two minutes over the bridge and we were completely surprised to find ourselves outside a huge Tesco's! It all seemed a bit bizarre and we had to go in, just out of interest. It was set out differently but clearly branded in exactly the same way. Still, at least it gave us the opportunity to restock our dry goods and pick up some cheese of the non-plastic variety. We were now more hopeful that we wouldn't be going hungry in Hungary or be existing purely on dry bread, plastic cheese and bright pink processed meat.

Although the weather improved greatly and the food marginally, the roads certainly did not. Apart from the odd riverside sections near towns, designated off-road cycle lanes disappeared completely, and even the painted-on-the-road lanes were no longer in existence. The EuroVelo 6 was not really a cycle route from this point, more a road that you could drive to the Black Sea on if you wanted. Of course, you could choose to take a bike instead of a car. If you were really lucky there might even be the occasional sign at the side of the dual carriageway which indicated it was indeed the bona fide bike route. Ridiculous! By the time we reached Budapest, we had been constantly harassed for days by fast-moving, hooting traffic of all shapes and sizes which had been passing us much too close for comfort. We were bags of nerves and were seriously considering alternative options. We might have set ourselves a challenge, one we were both keen to complete, but neither of us felt eagerly prepared to die in the process. That would just be stupid.

We were both looking forward to getting to Budapest. Firstly, it seemed like a significant milestone and achievement on our journey, secondly because neither of us had ever been there, and, thirdly everyone I spoke to who had been there described it as such a wonderful and clean place to visit, and they especially rated the thermal baths. As we approached, in early June, we were shocked by what we saw. On the streets, under the covered walkways, there were hundreds of homeless people; whole families with young children crowded together on a single blanket were sat next to drunk or drug-induced comatose young men in the next alcove.

There were also large numbers of elderly (mostly) men in wheelchairs with missing limbs or part limbs. Amongst the crowd, one man stumbled and shuffled towards us, in badly fitting slippers, with seeping, dirty bandages hanging off his legs. Our years of ambulance work meant we were familiar with the unique and disgusting rotting smell of leg ulcers. To be honest, it was one of the things that I was more than happy to leave behind and wished never to experience again. The crowd were clearly not expecting such an unpleasant aroma and we could see people understandably covering their faces, desperately trying not to vomit and attempting to move away from him as fast as possible. Guiltily, we too pedalled quickly away.

Huge six-foot-high piles of rubbish probably some 15 foot long were evident near nearly every major street junction. I can only describe the place as almost like a scene from an apocalyptic end-of-the-world motion picture. I expected and was prepared to see this type of abstract poverty when I visited India, but we were certainly not expecting to see anything even remotely like this in mainland Europe. It was a complete shock and left us feeling totally discombobulated. At this stage, we had no idea what was going on and wondered how on earth Hungary could possibly be being considered for full EU membership. There were serious social issues that needed urgently addressing here. It was a confusing and upsetting scene and we were puzzled.

This was in early June and the first TV reports in the UK about the building refugee crisis on mainland Europe were in August. Prior to this there had been some reports on the boat refugees tragically not making it across the Mediterranean on their crossings to Italy, but nothing (as far as I am aware) had been reported or was known about the sights we were unwittingly watching unfold.

After what we had seen we felt a tad guilty being able to book into a hotel for a couple of nights. However, our small penance I guess was that we had to carry our bikes and all of our luggage up two steep flights of stairs to the foyer area. There's a lot of effort involved in unloading and carrying multiple bags and bikes upstairs, and for this reason alone stopping on a campsite was often easier.

When the going was tough back in the early days, the thought that the kids we were raising money for couldn't just quit because life was difficult often helped to keep me motivated. Whilst we were still motivated to raise money for CHICKS, it didn't seem sensible at this stage to go and get knocked off our bikes and get ourselves killed in the process. So, over dinner we decided that the sensible thing was to change our route but ultimately cover the same mileage. That way we felt the charity wouldn't lose out just because we had bottled it. We decided our new route was to be into Croatia by train and then by bike to France via Venice and the lakes in Italy. We would no longer be heading to the Black Sea or in an easterly direction. We would get to Italy after all (which we obviously liked the idea of), but we would now be cycling over the Pyrenees mountains to make the challenge equal in distance but more difficult in content (which we hoped the people who had already kindly sponsored us would feel was a fair exchange).

The following morning, we heard from our son, who, at short notice, needed some crew for the boat he was moving from Greece to Turkey. Did we fancy it? Could we help him out? With flights booked as part of the package, no wages, just flights and food, it was just the cost-free break from the saddle that we felt we could do with, so we readily agreed. We arranged for Solo and Polo and all of our gear to be locked up in the basement of a cycle-hire shop for a tiny sum and hoped they would still be there on our return. We then visited the main Kiletti railway station in Budapest to book our train tickets to Croatia ready for our return.

After an hour of waiting in a queue, we were told by the short, round and very butch and grumpy lady behind the screen that we were at the wrong window. If we wanted to book tickets with bikes we had to go to the enquiry window, not the booking window. After another hour, we were told by the also short, but even more round and even more butch and grumpy, but this time moustachioed, lady that we could not take a train with a bike from Kiletti station at all and we would have to go to another station on the other side of the city. "No you cannot buy the ticket here. You will have to go there to buy it." We weren't convinced, as this was the main station, after all, and we decided to enquire at an alternative office on the other side of the platform. They would let us book tickets, but not for the bikes, and directed us to yet another enquiry office. This time we were told we needed to book a specific bike train. Only one or two left each day and we would have to go back and queue at (you guessed it) the original wrong window number one! Armed with a precious train number, we returned to Ms Grumpy's queue and another hour later, we were grudgingly issued with both people and bike tickets that we had the pleasure of paying for, whilst wondering if the cost of the tickets was somehow also docked from her wages, thus explaining her bad mood and obvious reluctance to sell them to us. The whole experience made British Rail in both its current and even old form seem positively efficient and an example of the highest possible standards of customer service.

With the little of what was now left of the day we visited the thermal baths and had a spin around the city to look at the main sites of Pest before heading off the next day to the airport. The city consists of two main parts, Buda on one side of the river and Pest on the other. The Buda side consists mainly of the old walled Fisherman's Quarter and a palace, all with stunning views of the Danube, the Parliament buildings opposite and the Chain Bridge which straddles across to the Pest side. There is more on the Pest side, a modern city with designer and high-street shops, hundreds of important historic buildings, statues, the Jewish Synagogue museum, the famous Ruin Bars (independently quirkily renovated funky bars in a previously almost derelict district) and most of the many thermal baths. We didn't really have time to see it all properly.

In a café in the Jewish quarter, we ordered a traditional Hungarian lunch, consisting of a starter of a wonderful soup made of sour cherries, cinnamon and crème fraiche and a main described badly as cauliflower stew but which was in actual fact delicious layers of minced beef, cheese sauce and cauliflowers with extra cheese on top, all for 500 florints. At the time there were 425 florints to the pound, so incredibly good value. We also found out from the very friendly owners that the city was experiencing a rubbish-collection strike. They didn't know anything about the homeless people as they didn't often go to that part of the city, but they thought a special free clinic had taken place for people without money yesterday, which might go some way to explain the large numbers of limbless people concentrated in one area. The next day, they assured us, the rubbish would be collected and the homeless people would return to cleaning the streets! Crikey, we thought, with that many cleaners, no wonder the city was normally described as spotless. It was all a bit surreal.

Chapter 21
Messing about on the water

Our brief encounter crewing on the boat began with us flying from Budapest to Chania on the Greek island of Crete, via Pisa in Italy. We arrived and spent a warm evening in the lively harbour town eating good food, drinking even better wine and catching up with Aaron's news. We were due to leave early the next morning as our destination was the island of Santorini 85 miles away.

Iain and I have both sailed a bit, though neither of us would consider ourselves experts and certainly not qualified beyond a competent crew level. Iain also used to be the operations director and business manager for a charity called the ICC (nothing to do with cricket). The Island Cruising Club was based on a decommissioned Mersey ferry permanently moored in the Salcombe Estuary, Devon, was a floating sailing activity centre which provided accommodation and sailing tuition (dinghies, yachts and motor boats) for both adults and children. It was a fantastic resource for budding new sailors, but sadly it no longer exists. What with us also living and working on outdoor adventure centres in a variety of locations across Europe, we both have plenty of general boat experience. As children, Aaron, his sister, Mairead, and our two Labrador dogs accompanied us on this more unusual existence and were lucky to experience and get excellent tuition, not just in skiing and sailing but canoeing, climbing, rafting, caving, kayaking, sea-kayaking, land-yachting and more. (And yes, before you think I've made a mistake, the dogs did it all too!) Aaron was particularly fond of and talented at skiing and did have a place on the British Junior Ski Team but decided against it when he realised it meant he no longer enjoyed skiing. Luckily, he was also particularly fond of and talented at sailing and decided to qualify to a high level and has made a successful career out of it, which meant at least one of us on board knew what they were doing.

We left port at 6am. Iain kindly offered to let me sleep in, but by 6.30am, I was awake and eager to be on deck. The sea was slightly choppy, and with me now up and about, Iain was able to nip below to make coffee. He came up looking a bit pale. Iain and Aaron love nothing more than a bit of wind-each-other-up banter. Iain was now taunted by Aaron saying things like "oh dear, are you feeling a little ittle wittle bit poorly?", "you look pukey", "oooo, you look pale. You are going to be sick, I can tell", "yep, you are definitely going to be sick, any minute now". Actually, he didn't look pale, he was a nasty shade of green, and I think I can now understand where the saying "green around the gills" comes from. A few minutes later, Iain did indeed have his head over the side and was projectile vomiting. Aaron was laughing SO much he actually had tears streaming down his face AND at times he could hardly breathe! I took a film of Aaron laughing at his dad's misfortune. Iain mistakenly still thinks it was in bad taste and that I was being mean by filming him vomiting.

Half an hour later, Iain was once again hanging over the side of the boat, puking with the same intensity. Aaron was crying with laughter again. I was laughing at Aaron laughing. I have never seen him in such hysterics. I feel I should point out Aaron is not an unkind person; if the tables had been turned and it was Aaron suffering from the same misfortune, Iain would most definitely be in tears of laughter too. They just have a mutual understanding whereby any piss-taking of the other is fair game, and this was a classic example. Clearly feeling a whole lot worse and definitely not feeling any better, Iain lay down on the deck of the boat in a fetal position and really helpfully went to sleep for the next ten hours. According to Aaron, in his experience, nearly everyone who is afflicted by serious sea-sickness ends up asleep on deck adopting this position.

So, for the next ten hours of fairly rough crossing, apart from the twenty magical minutes or so that we were accompanied by dolphins, Iain was asleep and useless. At one point he did wake up and declare, "I feel like a kid who doesn't know what to do with himself," and went back to sleep. He then needed a wee, but being unable to co-ordinate standing up and keeping his shorts out of the way of the aim, decided that removing his shorts completely would somehow make the task much easier! For some reason, Iain had difficulty understanding why it was no longer just Aaron in hysterical laughter. Thank goodness there were no other boats about.

Being a girl and needing a wee on a boat can be a bit of a palaver. I would wait as long as possible but had to go eventually, which, with the boat keeling over quite hard (almost on its side) and rocking up and down quite violently, meant there were lots of obstacles and bits of kit which had been thrown onto the floor. Getting from one end of the boat to the other below decks was like participating in some kind of giant moving obstacle course. It meant hanging onto the walls and cupboards on the way there to avoid being thrown off balance and then finally wedging myself in the head (which is boat-speak for loo – not my actual head!). With both feet and hands pushing hard against opposite walls in order to stay perched over the loo, it took a bit of skill to remain wedged and yet be relaxed enough elsewhere to actually wee!

On waking, Iain was a bit cross to discover that he had become sunburnt. We hadn't noticed his T-shirt was no longer covering a section of his back – probably something to do with us being a bit busy sailing for some reason – so he now had a large red stripe of burn across his lower back. For the last one-and-a-half hours of our thirteen-hour crossing Iain felt a bit better and took the helm, but not before he appeared from the aft (back) of the boat looking like Harry Potter, with a deep cut on his forehead and dripping blood all over the place. Somehow he had also managed to walk into the sun canopy!

We could see the clusters of bright white buildings clinging high up on the cliffs on the volcanic island of Santorini from some distance away. When we arrived, it was evident that there were no moorings to be had anywhere near the main port and we would have to attach to a buoy on the opposite side of the channel and go across by tender. We were all hungry and even Iain's appetite had returned. Our tender ride took half an hour longer than expected, due to a strong current, and we arrived just in time to find out that we could catch the last Santorini cable car up but there were no more coming down that evening. At least, we thought, we could get a lift up and eat sooner rather than later, and a walk down didn't really bother us.

A couple of hours later, hunger diminished and feeling the benefit of a few drinks, we began the long walk back down. The path was now used almost exclusively by donkeys whose owners are paid by lazy tourists to carry them up from the port to the clifftop town. We didn't see the donkeys as they don't work at night. Even in the dark, without the luxury of street lamps, however, we were well aware of their daytime presence, as we kept stepping in it. I'm pretty sure that the flip-flops and donkey poo on a surface of very worn and shiny cobbles in the pitch dark combination would send justified shivers of horror through every health and safety monitor in the land. It was treacherous, and we had to walk at a ridiculously slow speed, with thoughts of our cycling trip coming to a dramatic and sudden end due to donkey poo. Almost an hour later we reached the sanctuary of flat paths, lighting and the waterside.

Iain and Aaron walked down the appropriately named slipway and, well, slipped! In an instant, both of Iain's feet slipped forwards and the rest of him fell at full force and speed backwards, just before he landed his full weight onto his upper back and whiplashed his head onto the concrete surface, and slid at full speed into the water. Aaron tried to reach out and stop Iain's fall. However, rather than Aaron's help aiding Iain in any significant way, the momentum ensured that Aaron went over and slid into the water too. My instant thoughts were, "Shit! That could be a serious spinal or head injury. And if that is the case any available help would most likely be a long way away. Fuck! This really is not good." There were a few seconds in which I was seriously worried about the situation. Thankfully, although Iain was soaking wet, extremely bruised, concussed and had acquired yet another head cut, it seemed like he had got away without any serious damage. Aaron was fine too. Thankfully, I would not have to run/slide my way back up donkey-shit hill to summon help because, quite frankly, that would have been ridiculous and really not very quick.

After helping a dripping-wet, injured and now cold Iain back into the dinghy, we set off back to the yacht. If it hadn't been for a last-minute avoidance manoeuvre, which almost tipped us all overboard, Iain (at the front) might have also been decapitated by a large cruise ship mooring line. As if he hadn't already had enough misery for one day! This was only day one of our sailing excursion, and so far it wasn't really the type of relaxing break Iain had envisaged. Perhaps we should have just stuck to the bikes.

Chapter 22
Turkey

Many other islands
also exist!

Turkish
Mainland

Levitha

Self sufficient
goat island
Tualana

Turgutreis

Bodrum

Day 5

Day 3

Day 4

Kos Town

BIG trouble
with Anchor

Amorgos

Kos

Katapola Port

Day 2

Anchored

Donkey poo path down from Fira

Santorini

OLD PORT Sea sick!
Ian stopped me step away

Dolphins

Day 1

Ian sea sick!

Certainly NOT to scale
or even anywhere near it!

Chania (port)

Crete

The following day we sailed about 40 miles to Amorgos, another of the Greek Cyclade islands. The crossing was a bit rough again, and preparing lunch wedged in the galley (kitchen) was no easy feat. Compared, however, to mooring up that evening, it was much more simple. Most moorings in this part of the world seem to favour the fore (front) or aft (rear) part of the boat being attached to the land. In the UK, most moorings are arranged so that you tie the boat up alongside. Anyway, we were directed to the last mooring, but it was debatable as to whether this was deep enough for the boat. We had a look and Aaron decided it wasn't. We were offered another mooring further up the coast, where the current and wind were stronger and the tyres on the wall would damage the boat, so we declined. There was one other particularly narrow mooring between two other boats, into which we could fit, but it would require a bit of skill. Aaron was confident it would not be a problem. Before backing into these aft moorings, an anchor is thrown out, which both secures the boat from the fore end and gives some additional control of the boat before arriving landside and tying the aft.

In UK ports it is common for people to just watch when someone else moors, often commenting to each other how they could have done it better, but not becoming involved. In Mediterranean ports it is much more common for everyone, from boat owners to passing tourists to the milkman, to shout loudly, dishing out unwanted advice and to become involved, mostly causing chaos and a tangle of lines, or worse. Luckily, we were aware of this unusual etiquette and would only listen to our skipper when mooring. When our anchor chain jammed, it was almost impossible to control the boat into the unusually narrow space in the normal manner. The onlooking and involved crowd of fellow boat owners, shopkeepers, restaurateurs, tourists, milkmen and policemen were shouting pass me a rope, give me a this, pass me a that, do it this way, do it that way, totally unaware and oblivious that this could be no ordinary mooring. Whilst Aaron was busy trying calmly to unjam the chain, Iain and I were busy fending off, as the current was desperately trying to push us against the neighbouring boat. Understandably, the owners of the neighbouring boat were equally concerned and were also totally consumed with fending off. Meanwhile, the rest of the island had now gathered and were shouting, screaming and trying to be involved. Eventually, Iain told them all to fuck off, couldn't they see there was a mechanical issue? If they could help with fending off that would be useful, but stop chucking bloody ropes and shouting. Obviously not understanding a single word he said, they took no notice whatsoever and just continued shouting! With the help of another boat owner who could see what the issue was, they finally freed the anchor and managed to moor. It was all a bit fraught, to say the least, and was one of those occasions on a boat when you wished you knew a bit more and could be a bit more helpful. It made me miss the simplicity of our own trip and the bikes.

Our next stop was the island of Lisoi, which was an absolute unspoilt dream. Owned and occupied by the same family for 700 years, they supported themselves by running a small taverna serving simple meals made from their own sheep, goats, cheese, fruit, vegetables and local fish. The island was totally self-sufficient, with their own water supply and solar electric panels. The only way onto the island was by boat, and we were lucky enough to secure one of the few moorings. It was a real treat, and this time we even thought to take a torch for the walk back along the goat path, and we managed an entire day without either stepping in poo or being involved in incidents or accidents.

We then sailed on to Kos, a complete contrast: overcrowded, over-run with bars, processed food galore and more. Poverty was also evident and there were countless homeless people, including children, begging for food. Was this a result of the economic crisis in Greece? we wondered. Iain and Aaron had some trouble with an overly officious official when trying to present the boat papers and passports (for the following day's voyage across to Turkey) before they had finished dealing with the hundreds of passengers due out on the tourist booze cruise, and as a result, had first to wait an hour and were then told to come back after lunch. Oh, the power!

The journey across from Kos to Turgutreis in Turkey was rough and fairly unpleasant. Luckily, Iain had now gained his sea-legs and was no longer feeling seasick, and we were across in a couple of hours, assisted by good sails and the back-up of a reliable engine should we need it. We later learned that this was the same passage (in reverse) that thousands of Syrian refugees attempted in unsuitable and unseaworthy rubber dinghies. Weeks later, the shores of both Greece and Turkey would be littered with hundreds of washed-up useless lifejackets and deflated dinghies. Another part of the Mediterranean Sea would become an unwelcome and premature watery tomb for desperate people, including children.

After hours of cleaning, scrubbing and de-salting in 40°C heat, which were all unpleasant but annoyingly necessary chores on a wooden yacht which was about to be left moored for some time, we were set free to use the marina's facilities, which included a long and very welcome swim in a magnificently cool blue pool. Refreshed and now cleaner than we had been for days, we ordered gin and tonics and planned what to do the next day before flying back to Budapest to continue our cycle tour. We decided on another swim, a look around the local shopping area, and, for Iain, a real Turkish barber experience, before there was any chance that I might have to cut his hair again.

Aaron and I caught up with Iain at the barber's just as he was being oiled with about the tenth different-smelling potion and was enjoying a neck massage. He didn't look quite so pleased when later on his head was being thrown from side to side! But overall, he was extremely impressed by the haircut itself and thoroughly enjoyed the pampering experience. It cost him an incredibly tiny amount of money and he wished he could always fly there to get his hair cut. With the price some hairdresser's charge in the UK, it could possibly become a viable option.

We were both now looking forward to getting back on the bikes, and although the sailing trip had not really been a rest, especially for Iain(!), it had been lovely to see the sea again, and the experience had definitely been the change we had needed. Several times throughout the sailing trip, we had discussed and revisited our decision to change our cycle route. On one hand, our choice of route change did seem perfectly rational, but it was always accompanied by an undercurrent of guilty feelings or a sense of failure, despite still intending to cover the same distance. Eventually, we decided that even though we had already purchased the train tickets to Croatia, we would now not be using them and instead we would "man up" and continue to the Black Sea after all.

It had been great spending time with Aaron, and as usual, it was upsetting to be parting again. We all shared a taxi to Bodrum airport, and whilst Aaron flew home to Nice in France, we flew back to Budapest, this time via Istanbul. At Istanbul airport, in a line for checking in to Baghdad, we saw a man with a crossbow complete with arrows.

We were keen to get back cycling again and were hoping that our bikes and luggage were still where we had left them.

Chapter 23
Swarms

Thankfully the bikes and luggage were all intact, and we set off with renewed optimism through the traffic of Budapest and on towards a town called Baja. We stocked up on food in town and made our way to a campsite on the banks of the River Danube. With a triathlon event being held, the town and riverside was a mass of competitors and spectators, and there was a lively happy atmosphere with plenty of inspirational music clips and announcements being played over the loudspeakers. We pitched our tent on the campsite, which was also the local sports amenity. That evening, a wedding reception was being celebrated in the sports hall. At midnight the music from the motivating disco music across the river at the triathlon event was competing with the Hungarian equivalent of the Birdy Song music being played at the wedding and the techno music from the school prom disco on the opposite side of the road. Our tent was equidistant from each event, resulting in a rather loud and shit musical mix. Just as we thought it couldn't get worse, the youth in cars (clearly not invited into the school prom disco) were showing off their skidding skills in the car park opposite. At no time did any of this seem threatening or dangerous, it just seemed like lots of people having fun and taking part in a "we can make more noise than you" competition. This all meant we weren't likely to get any sleep, even with earplugs. At about 2am, just as the music began to die down from all directions, there was a sudden and loud rendition by a bugle of something very similar to the last post, and just as suddenly, it all went quiet. It was quite surreal, most welcome and fairly amusing. We didn't find it quite so welcome and were definitely not quite so amused when it was repeated at 6am.

The following day we were impressed by and made huge progress on the wonderfully smooth designated bike lane which headed out of town. We were now easily covering distances only dreamed of in the earlier days and all without triggering pain or ailments. The weather was good, we were off road and feeling that our decision to get back onto the original route was the right one. After lunch, however, we became a little concerned as we didn't seem to have come across the town we were expecting to pass through. In fact, we weren't passing through anywhere, just mile upon mile of wonderful track through the middle of nowhere (beautiful countryside, but nowhere nonetheless). Eventually, we came across a bar and established that we were nowhere that was on our map. In our excitement at finding the first "proper" cycle path that we had seen for some considerable time, we had wrongly assumed that it was the EuroVelo6 and was going in our direction! It was doing neither. Because of our "strip section" maps (which only showed a couple of kilometres either side of the actual route), we had no option but to turn around and go back to where we started. Hurrah, another night accompanied by the bugle.

The following day, we tried again. We discovered the route was back on a main road and headed back into town to buy some fluorescent and reflective tabards to wear. We then spent the day being harassed by traffic passing us too fast and too close for our liking. By the evening we were not so sure that we had made the right decision to carry on. Emails from both Crazy Harry and Johnny and from Mateus and Fanny, who were both ahead of us, described it getting worse, and both couples were now having issues with bad signage, bad surfaces, being chased by dogs, and finding places to stay, and both had had close shaves with traffic.

Iain and I differ (as I am sure most couples do). Iain seemed to want to find out every possible detail of everything that could possibly go wrong, in order to prepare for every possible situation. From my perspective, this just seemed to fuel unnecessary panic and fear and served no practical purpose. I preferred not to hear reports from further up the track. I would rather have an optimistic view of what was to come and be aware of the dangers in the background, not the foreground. We had a difference of opinion (read row), when Iain said we should have taken the train and the alternative route after all. He was also terrified that my bike, which was "clearly too big" (shock, horror!), "made me particularly unstable and wobbly when passed by traffic". Obviously, I didn't have a death wish, but did want to continue and thought it stupid that he hadn't expressed his excessive feelings of fear before making the decision to carry on. If we died now, it would all be my fault, and another set of train tickets would be expensive. I was also pretty pissed off that he had not previously bothered to mention that he too did in actual fact believe my bike WAS TOO BIG and had always held this opinion! We came to a compromise: we would carry on and if either of us thought we were experiencing actual and present danger (and not just the possibility of future dangers) the other would agree that we should get on a train and avoid that section. We would make up the difference in mileage at the end of the trip with a jaunt along the Black Sea coast.

So, the following day, we set off again, him on his appropriately sized bike and me on my ridiculously far-too-large-to-be-safe one. We stopped to eat lunch, which consisted of some fresh bread rolls and cakes that we had bought at a baker's and some more plastic orange cheese with bright red processed sausage meat. The rolls were a little dry, but we had become used to that. The fruit in what we thought were scones turned out to be lumps of hard and chewy fat, so not quite the sweet treat we were hoping for, winning the award for "the most disgusting and disappointing cake of the entire trip".

As we cycled through some pretty countryside I noticed that Iain was being accompanied by what looked like several bees. After a few crashed into my uncovered shoulders, I looked around and realised I had attracted an even larger crowd; dozens seemed to be swarming around extra-large Polo and me. I shouted "Bees – go faster!" to Iain, and for once, he heard me and increased the pace. But the bees kept up. Realising they were keeping up, I shouted, "You need to go even faster", but this time there was no response. I guessed that as he only had a few dozen around him and his shoulders were covered he probably didn't feel he was in any danger. I, however, now had a full-on "buzzing cartoon cloud" of at least a hundred flying insects taking kamikaze dives at my head, face and shoulders. I decided to take evasive action and overtake Iain, and so I pedalled as fast as my little legs would carry me, which incidentally turned out to be not fast enough to outrun these flying devils. Iain now realised why I had been shouting for him to speed up and was astonished at the sheer numbers of insects now surrounding and dive-bombing us both. Luckily, a car passing in the opposite attention attracted the insects' attention and the swarm decided to follow it instead of us.

They weren't bees, but these unpleasant and unknown biting insects dive-bombed and harassed us for the rest of the day, hanging around us and increasing in swarm size each time, until a more attractive and faster-moving vehicle of any description came along. It was the first day we were willing and praying for additional traffic on the road. The insects turned what would have otherwise been a beautiful section into a hostile environment.

When heading for a campsite marked on our map we followed another bike-touring couple, the first we had seen for a long time, as most other EV6 tourers finish their journey at Budapest. They were only a few hundred metres in front of us, and an elderly man was waving, nodding and pointing in the direction of a small pathway through the trees, along the bank of the river. As we passed the gentleman, he waved, nodded and pointed for us too. This was encouraging as this was where our map showed the campsite to be and, as you are aware, the maps were turning out to be a tad unreliable at times. As we followed and caught up with the couple (who we discovered were French), it became evident to us all that there was no campsite. The owners of a couple of holiday chalets confirmed there was no campsite but said that we could pitch up on the grass verge if we liked. They were kind enough, too, to bring us some water and offer us fruit juice.

As we pitched up we were annoyed by a few mosquitos. We all took evasive action and put on extra layers of clothes. These were no ordinary mozzies, they were drawing blood through the French lady's denim jeans! We spent the early evening wearing multiple layers of clothes, including pillow cases and sarongs around our faces and over our heads and with plastic bags over our feet because they could also bite through trainers. Seeing as the temperature was still over 40°C, we were wearing far too many clothes, and with these buggers intent on biting us as much as possible, it was a particularly unpleasant evening. The thought of some nice food cheered us up. We had bought some fresh salad (which had not been common to come by), and whilst under attack, we prepared and cooked onions, garlic and bacon lardons to accompany it. When we tipped the cooked lardon mixture on top of the salad, it became immediately covered in a thick living layer of the nasty black insects, rendering the meal inedible. With dinner ruined and being bitten at an unpleasant rate, we had no option but to retreat into the tent for the night, where we spent at least an hour trying unsuccessfully to eradicate any mosquito that had sneaked in with us. With nothing to eat but our previously unfavoured lunch delicacies – yum more fat-filled scones – we spent an uncomfortably hot and extremely itchy, sleepless night and emerged in the morning looking like the male and female versions of the Elephant Man.

Chapter 24
Country number seven

The only plus coming from staying in Mosquito Metropolis was that we were suddenly able to pack up and move out within 20 minutes, a record-breaking time. With more than twenty bites already on my forehead, three of which were the size of ping-pong balls, I was keen not to collect any more. The French couple had already packed up and left us a note saying to join them for breakfast on the other side of the river.

Iain managed to arrive just before the ferry back across the river was due to leave and waited for me to catch up with his front wheel on the ramp. I was only a minute or so behind him. At the exact time the ferry was scheduled to leave, Iain was told to either get on the ferry or get off the ramp. He pointed to me, by now just at the top of the slipway, to which the ferry operator shook his head and indicated for Iain to remove his bike from the ramp. Somehow as Iain reversed, his bike became unbalanced and promptly fell heavily over onto its side onto the slipway. The hurriedly departing boat then deposited a nice wave of river water all over the breached bike. Now, if anyone else had actually been on the boat or there had been anyone waiting on the other side of the river for the boat, we might have been a bit understanding about them being sticklers for the timetable. But there weren't, which made the whole incident even more annoying. Luckily, our bags were all waterproof, but we were annoyed at having to now spend a pointless half hour waiting on a mosquito-infested river bank for an empty ferry to come back, whilst having the pleasure of collecting yet more bites and knowing we would now miss both breakfast and the other cycle tourers.

The previous night we had decided once again to quit. Once again, in the light of day we changed our minds and decided to carry on. We couldn't quite figure out exactly why we kept deciding to carry on; we'd always said we would stop if either of us felt we were no longer enjoying the experience. There had been nothing enjoyable whatsoever about the previous night. The meal was ruined, we didn't have enough food, there were no facilities, we were bitten to pieces, it was hot and uncomfortable, we were disturbed all night by buzzing mosquitos, we got no sleep whatsoever, we were tired, hungry, miserable and knackered. Before we left the UK, we'd decided we wouldn't make vital decisions if tired, hungry or ill, which is why we reviewed the previous night's decision to quit over a substandard, although exceptionally cheap, breakfast of pastries (which was all we could find). We discussed why we kept wanting to carry on, despite not currently enjoying the experience, and concluded that we had come SO far, we could almost see the finish line, and it would be a real shame not to complete the challenge now. Changing route was still an option, if necessary for safety reasons, but other than that, we were now, once again, expecting to make it to the Black Sea.

For once, our maps gave us a pleasant surprise. We were expecting an "unmade" surface (read Brighton beach) and were instead presented with lovely smooth tarmac to cycle on. We enjoyed several miles along a lovely peaceful levy where we saw many black and white storks and could hear other birds singing. Subsistence farming was widely evident from the presence of the many old women tending to their crops with hand tools. Maybe they weren't old in reality, but they definitely all looked at least 90 years old, bent over double with their headscarf-clad heads, toothless grins and long flowing skirts. It was like a scene depicting medieval Britain from a child's school history book. We were then flung straight back out into the twenty-first century as the route took us back onto a main road, which luckily had a designated cycle lane and meant we were at least slightly separated from the screaming trucks and speeding traffic. Well, it did for a couple of miles anyway, and then the cycle lane just ceased to exist.

So often on this trip we had noticed that one minute everything was great and the next it was the total opposite. During the several thousand kilometres covered to date we discussed this numerous times and decided that it was mostly due to being totally unable to control our own destiny. Yes, we had learnt some tricks to help us along, like if you see a shop buy your dinner, no matter what time of day it is. Carrying it knowing you have it with you is easier and much better than either going hungry or doing extra miles at the end of the day to try and find some. But on the whole, other than injury, whether the cycling was good or bad was down to weather, surface or other traffic, and all of these were beyond our control. Our lives had been stripped down to the real bare essentials, and as such, we had become much more affected by our surroundings than we would previously have thought possible. On the whole, this was a pleasurable but completely unpredictable experience which we learnt required a positive mental attitude in order to cope with it.

Being overtaken by screaming truck after screaming truck for mile after mile after mile not only wore out our positive mental attitudes but also proved to be physically exhausting too. Every time a truck passed it was essential to keep the handlebars in a vice-like grip, in order to stop the bike being sucked under the truck wheels. The adrenaline produced by the fear of being sucked under a truck's wheels also seemed to make us pedal faster, which made us tire quicker and feel exceedingly hungry. By the time we reached the Croatian border crossing, both of our arms, shoulders and legs felt like they were going to fall off, and we were shattered and hungry again.

The Croatian border control lady, impressed by our journey so far, happily stamped our passports (despite not really needing to) and encouraged the (previously grumpy) Hungarian border man to do the same. Sadly, there were no "bike" picture stamps, only "car" ones, so we got one of those each and, after the obligatory border-crossing photos, we got back on our bikes and once again joined the traffic.

Thankfully, after a short distance we were once again back on smaller, quieter roads, but just to make sure we were still challenged, we picked up a nice strong head-wind. Iain and I chatted and created a league table of our worst conditions. We both agreed heavy traffic was all-time number one. For second place we differed. I thought bad surface was more difficult to deal with than head-wind, and Iain thought head-wind was worse and more demoralising than bad surface, although, to be fair, we both said there wasn't really much in it, so awarded a joint second place to head-wind and Brighton beach surface. Third place went to extended periods of rain and fourth to unnecessary barriers. Fifth was jointly won by shit maps and crap signage.

Our mobile phone company was not allowed on the list, as it couldn't really be described as a cycling condition. However, it was the thing causing us the most hassle. We had specifically taken it along for use in an emergency and to contact family. It obviously needed to be suitable for use across our entire route, which is why we chose a Lebara roaming phone for Europe and explained to the company what we were doing. We accumulated 46 euros of credit, which had to be used within 28 days, but were unable to "activate" it unless we were back in the UK. We phoned the company several times and explained that we were on a charity cycle ride and that we were travelling across Europe, and we appealed to their better nature to "activate" our accumulated credit. They declined, stating it was impossible to "activate" it whilst we were abroad. Funnily enough, they were still able to take and "activate" further payments from us whilst we were abroad. Shame on you, Lebara.

The people of Croatia seemed on the whole to be very friendly towards us. We even had people calling out and wishing us good luck, for some reason mostly in French (not sure why?). Our trip took us through some beautiful countryside and more modern farming was evident compared to what we had seen in Hungary. Although now on smaller roads, surrounded by stunning countryside, we were encountering many hills and realised we had left hills off the worst conditions list and they really should also be on it somewhere very near to the bloody top! Each valley seemed to have a charming little village nestled in it, but unfortunately each time the road approached a village, it narrowed substantially and remained narrow both through the village and on the killer steep hill up on the way out. This meant that as well as being almost impossible to actually cycle the killer steep uphill gradient, it was actually impossible for other traffic to overtake us safely. As a consequence, we were either overtaken unsafely or not overtaken at all and collected a very long, and I'm sure, very unhappy line of extremely slow-moving traffic.

At the top of one such killer hill, Iain somehow had the energy to both wave and ding his bell at a small child being held by his mother at the entrance to a farm. Before I reached them she had run into the farm and re-emerged running towards me with the gift of two freshly picked peaches. What a lovely gesture and, of course, after the hill we had just climbed, they were simply the best peaches either of us had ever tasted. She was waiting for her husband and other family to come back for lunch on their tractors and she would make sure they would check we were OK later. I'm not sure if this kind thought worried or reassured us, but, sure enough, for the rest of the day every tractor driver in the area seemed to give us a friendly wave.

There was still plenty of evidence, in the form of bullet and blast holes in the masonry of many buildings, of the war between the countries of the former Yugoslavia in the area near the Croatia–Serbia border. In the countryside villages we also noticed many neglected and overgrown properties which looked like they had been abandoned long ago and not used or lived in since. Most of these properties also had a blue bag hanging on the perimeter fence. We have been unable to find out the significance (if any) of the blue bags. We were warned by locals not to wander off the designated routes in the countryside as there was still the possibility of stepping on landmines. We did as we were told! Unsurprisingly, there were no campsites in this area. Luckily, pensions (B&Bs), including the biggest breakfast we had ever come across, were cheaper than the cost of a German or Austrian campsite. Staying in rooms for a few nights also had the added bonus of keeping us out of the reach of the vampire mosquitos, and not having to set up camp, and especially not having to pack up, gave us extra valuable cycling time.

After a huge breakfast consisting of a mountain of scrambled eggs, three loaves of bread, butter, jam, a plate of dried meats (some very spicy) the size of a lorry wheel, a plate of cheese the same size as the meat, tomatoes, tea, coffee and some elderflower cordial so sweet it could actually remove tooth enamel, and after trying, once again unsuccessfully, to top up our phone (this time the website was down), we set off with nothing but an unusable 46 euro phone credit, straight back onto the busy main road, feeling nervous (hoping that the emergency number 112 was free like 999 is in the UK), towards a town called Vukovar.

Chapter 25
Serbia

One morning, alongside the Danube in a park in Croatia, close to the town of Olisjek, I watched a pug dog deliberately position his bottom so as to expertly place a perfectly formed walnut-whip-shaped poo dead centre on the top of a mole hill! There's not really anything else to add to that, other than when on a cycle tour, you really can't tell what you might see next.

On the whole, we had a great day on the bikes. There was hardly any traffic on the road and we made great progress.

It was eerie, as we entered Vukovar, there was still no traffic on the road, where normally we'd expect it to increase on the approach to a town. The town had significantly more battle scars than any we had previously passed through too. There was a water tower on the hill, which had great chunks missing and huge holes right through it. It looked as if it might fall over at any minute. The town was quiet too, and we had a bit of difficulty finding somewhere to stay within our budget and, as usual, we ended up making a couple of pointless trips up unnecessary hills. Finally, we came across a pension, owned by Boris (not making it up), quite possibly the tallest man with the biggest hands and the deepest voice that I had ever come across. He informed us that it was Croatian Independence Day, which was why the roads were quiet. "Don't worry," he said, "it will all be back to normal tomorrow." "Great," we replied, not wishing to disagree with a man of such proportions. Actually, he was a really nice guy and went on to tell us that most people now wish to forget the recent(ish) conflict (1990s), that he had lost friends, both Serbian and Croatian, and the familiar story that amongst normal citizens there had been no winners. Croatian Independence Day was not a celebration as such, more a day of quiet reflection.

We went off to town to find some food and came across double-scoop ice creams at just one euro each, so made a start with one of them. Due to the holiday, there were only a couple of shops open and so we stocked up on some bread, ham and cheese, just for a change. The only wine Iain could find was a Tetra Pak carton and I both took photos and ribbed him endlessly for buying it (normally even a screw top is too inferior a wine for Mr A). "Didn't they have a brown paper bag for you as well?" I mocked.

We then came across the memorial gardens and cemetery for the town of Vukovar and it was then that we realised why the name was familiar. In August 1991 the Serbians had attacked Vukovar. The Croatian town managed to hold off an invasion for three months. The town suffered terrible bombardment during this time and much of it was destroyed. In November the Serbians besieged the town and then captured and took over 5,000 Vukovar citizens to concentration camps in Serbia. Reports that severe atrocities were being committed were later confirmed. We remembered seeing the BBC news footage of emaciated prisoners with arms through the boundary fence, looking almost identical to footage of Japanese prisoners of World War Two, and being horrified that this had happened in

Europe in the late twentieth century. Hardly any of the 5,000 men and boys returned. Many of the dead are only now being discovered and recovered some twenty-five years later. The memorial garden had a simple white cross for each of the 5,000 victims plus a cemetery packed with almost identical black headstones. It was a poignant and sobering visit; almost all of the victims were the same age as or younger than us.

One hour later, we were in the cinema watching the latest Jurassic Park film! In our defence, feeling quite affected by the memorial, we didn't want to go back and just sit in our room for the whole evening. There was nothing else open, and (last but by no means least) Jurassic Park was the only film on offer. It was, however, in English, so at least we didn't have to read the subtitles. It was a stark contrast to what we had been doing earlier in the day, but it did further confirm what a bunch of dicks humans can be, due mostly to power and greed, or sometimes disguised as the will of some (most probably) imaginary higher being, especially when in possession of weapons, technology or dinosaurs.

Setting off early for breakfast, we discovered that you could buy drinks in the cafés in Vukovar, but not breakfast. We chose several interesting-looking pastries at the baker's and enjoyed all of them, except the deep-fried one which contained lumps of unidentifiable meat, most of which were fat. The sausage and fruit ones (not together – that would be odd), although a bit dry, were delicious once dunked into coffee (not the sausage one – that would also be weird).

The roads were, as predicted by Boris, once again busy but often had a decent empty pedestrian pathway, which we took advantage of. We discovered that the parts of Croatia that we passed through had bakers which sold a wonderful variety of bread rolls which were available pre-made with a range of very generous portions of tasty fillings and probably cheaper than making them yourself. They were the perfect lunch option and in Ilok we ate our rolls on a Roman ruin perched on the top of a hill overlooking the Danube. Just as we set off again, it began to rain and did so for the rest of that day.

Just before we crossed into Serbia, we met another cycle tourist travelling in the opposite direction to us. Obligatory sizing up completed, we learnt he was a Scottish guy, who had started in Greece, had been through Turkey and Bulgaria and was heading to Norway. He had heard of us from "the other" English couple (of iron bar fame), who were just a couple of days ahead of us, and it wasn't until he met them that he worked out that there were in fact two English couples heading on the same route at the same sort of time. Prior to working this out, he had unsurprisingly encountered trouble creating a cohesive image of what the amalgamated English couple would look like! (We could not look more different, are of different ages, have different bikes, tents, accents, and we didn't have an iron bar!) He had not come across Crazy Harry and

Johnny but had heard of them. It was like a strange moving community, where your reputation unknowingly precedes your actual arrival. We then each exchanged tips on the route ahead and emptied our pockets, exchanging our Croatian for his Serbian change. In that respect, it was really useful coming across someone so near to a border crossing.

We passed through the dismal and run-down Serbian border, gaining another stamp in our passports. It really was just like the good old days. The duty-free shop was dilapidated, empty and looked as if it had closed decades ago. By now it was raining heavily and we were soaked through to the skin. The route was back on the main roads, and in addition to the usual traffic hazards, we now had road spray, poor visibility and skidding to consider. Our journey into the first town over the border was quite possibly one of the most miserable of the trip. We headed towards the train station, thinking that this was probably the most likely place to find a hotel or somewhere to stay. We stopped to ask directions and drew quite an excitable and very friendly crowd. Several people spoke a little English but none of them seemed to know where the station was. Eventually, one of them managed to explain that the station had closed six, seven, maybe even ten years ago! They were trying to piece together directions for the next one which was miles away. We explained that we were heading towards Novi-Sad and they eagerly gave us directions to there, and we less eagerly decided to push on. Before we left town we called into a great little cycle shop, run by a Serbian motorbike champion, to give our bikes a quick service. His lovely girlfriend spoke English very well and told us she had recently returned early from studying in Germany because she didn't feel welcome. She described them as "no smile" people. They (the bike shop people, not the Germans) were horrified that we were intent on cycling between Novi-Sad and Belgrade and described it as too dangerous, with crazy fast drivers who don't like bikes, much bigger roads with many lanes. This concerned us greatly, and we set off in silence towards Novi-Sad.

Chapter 26
The train

At Novi-Sad we used the internet and found out the following. The other English couple had taken a back route to avoid the traffic into Belgrade and in the mud she had fallen off her bike and broken her arm. They were now on the way home. The Americans, Crazy Harry and Johnny, had been seriously shaken up by the traffic, had taken a couple of trains to get away from it and were now in Romania having an awful time being harassed and chased by packs of wild dogs. We also heard that a Spanish couple (we hadn't met but had heard of) had also been chased by dogs but, more seriously, had been robbed of all their belongings at knife point in Romania. The French couple were now heading south to Montenegro but described the approach into Belgrade as being horrendous.

Neither of us fancied much more bad traffic, dogs and least of all being robbed at knife point. We got out the maps to look for alternative routes. We settled on an overnight train from Belgrade to Sofia (Bulgaria), which would take us further south, hopefully into warmer, less wet weather. We would then continue to cycle east and hit the Black Sea at a place called Varna. The prospect of an overnight train seemed to add even more adventure and a bit more interest to our journey, so we were pleased with our decision. We just had the small matter of getting to Belgrade.

As warned, the main road into Belgrade was indeed horrendous, and we would have both preferred to have been poked in the eyes with sharp sticks. When a taxi stopped to offer us a lift, we jumped at the chance. Luckily for us (and maybe this is why he stopped), our driver had bike bars on his roof. With some considerable time spent fiddling about, we managed to secure our bikes and get the luggage safely in the boot, all whilst being unpleasantly soaked to the skin by speeding traffic spray.

Our driver seemed to be the Serbian equivalent of a cross between Arthur Daley and Del Boy. Perhaps knowing the route was an unsuitable cycle route and knowing he would find distressed cyclists every now and again was the real reason he had a cycle rack on his car. He didn't really look like a cyclist, after all! He was currently making and exporting car air-fresheners to Russia. "Could we smell them?" Not only could we smell them, we could taste them. They were making our eyes water and they were in the front of the car and we were in the back. He explained that he would prefer Serbia to become more closely allied with Russia than become more involved with the EU "and all of its crazy, not necessary, health and safety rules". He was a very likeable and lively character who explained he just loved meeting people from different parts of the world and getting new business ideas from them. We suggested that he might consider opening a campsite for cycle tourists and he really seemed to like the idea. By the time we had left the car, despite still driving, he had drawn a plan of one and had called a man about a piece of land he knew was for sale cheap. He had even drawn on where he would play his guitar in order to entertain his guests and salvaged a washing machine from a closing-down launderette. On parting, we wished him every success and often wonder what he might be up to now; it really could be anything.

The area around the train station at Belgrade was crowded, full of mostly young men seemingly hanging around without a real purpose. We were wary and for the first time, I think, a bit concerned that our belongings might be stolen. In its original state the station would have been quite grand. The queuing space to each booking window was separated by a carved dark wood palisade upon which you could fill out a cheque or sort out your money whilst waiting for your turn to be served. Inside the station, only one window was open to buy international tickets. Each and every other queuing strip contained a homeless family, including many children, sitting on the floor on a blanket. We bought our tickets, but weirdly, although we were allowed to take our bikes on board, we could not pay for them in advance and would have to pay the guard direct, and no, she didn't know how much that would be! In the couple of hours we had before the train set off we found a hotel with secure parking for Solo and Polo in which to have some dinner. We also managed to find out from the waiter roughly what we should expect to pay for the carriage of our bikes.

Back at the station, we wheeled our bikes straight through to the platform, thinking it would be less crowded and perhaps safer than on the concourse. It wasn't, and we were immediately confronted by a platform completely covered by sleeping bodies; it would have been impossible to squeeze another one on, it was that crowded. Luckily, we were heading out of a different platform because there was no way we could have negotiated a path through. Once again, we misinterpreted the situation and thought (this time) that Serbia had serious homeless and social issues.

When our graffiti-covered, communist-era train arrived, it didn't look too promising and was nothing like the romantic image of a night train that I had envisaged. Firstly, we had to find the guard and get his permission to board the bikes. Luckily this went well and he was most helpful. The sleeper train consisted of dozens of sleeping compartments, each containing six berths, three on each side, and between the two sets of triple bunks a door opened onto the carriage corridor. It was obvious that not one single part of the train had ever been cleaned, washed or even wiped since it went into service decades ago. It was disgusting. Even the trains I took in India were substantially cleaner. You could only book a bed (not an entire compartment), and therefore, unless travelling in a handy group of six, you would undoubtedly be sharing your compartment with complete strangers.

We were allocated compartment number seven, which was inconveniently placed at the far end of the corridor. Our bikes, we were informed, would have to be in the compartment with us, for which we were extremely grateful. Not only would we be able to keep an eye on them, but it also prevented anyone else from joining us in our compartment. Result! We now just had the awkward task of getting our bikes and luggage safely onto the train without leaving anything unattended! The farce went something like this. We unhitched Iain's luggage from his bike, as near to the train door as possible without being in the way, and placed it next to my bike. Whilst watching both my bike and all the luggage, Iain went backwards up three ridiculously steep steps which were five foot high in total, whilst carrying the front of his bike, I carried up the rear until the bike was on the train and then quickly returned to my bike and Iain's luggage. Iain then had to manoeuvre the bike around the bend, into and along the corridor, simultaneously trying to get past numerous backpackers negotiating how to squeeze six grown adults and their oversized backpacks into such a small sleeping compartment, and finally he wheeled the bike into our own ridiculously small sleeping compartment, first having to fold up and secure the lower bunk beds out of the way. Meanwhile, I was unclipping the luggage from my bike, wondering why he was taking so long, and worrying because the train was due to leave in less than five minutes. He then returned to do the same with my bike (have I mentioned that, as well as being too big, it is also heavier than his?). Back at the train door we began loading our ten bags. First we tried just piling them all up to the top of the stairs, but this blocked the entrance, which didn't go down well with the backpackers, so Iain ended up taking a few more trips along the corridor. All this we completed with seconds to spare as the train sounded its horn and crept out of the station.

A few minutes after setting off, our door opened and we were each thrown a dirty, scratchy blanket, a filthy, non-covered pillow and an old and torn, but at least clean, single sheet. What was the point in the single clean sheet? we wondered. Were we supposed to put it on top of the filthy bed and then use a filthy blanket? What was the point in that? Or were we somehow supposed to wrap it around us protecting us from both bed and blanket? We decided on covering the manky bed with the clean sheet, depositing both the dirty blanket and pillow on the unused bunk and using our own bedding. I can't even begin to describe how bad the toilet was.

The train was hot. Thank goodness there were only the two of us in our compartment. I dread to think how hot the compartment next to us, occupied by five young American and one British guy, was. Initially, we started with our window open, but our driver seemed to favour the excessive use of the horn and it kept us awake. At one point I thought I was dreaming, perhaps prompted by being thrown bedding earlier. The train had stopped and I could hear people shouting and asking for water. Had I been transported back to World War Two? It must be a dream. I also heard an American voice asking "Where have you come from, buddy?" and en masse a group of people replied "Syria". Now realising this wasn't a dream, and putting together sights previously seen in Budapest and Belgrade, it all began to make sense. We had been witnessing the beginnings of a huge refugee exodus across Europe from Syria. At this stage the numbers were in the hundreds; they would soon become hundreds of thousands.

We spent the rest of the journey sometimes drifting into sleep, but mostly not. At 5am the train stopped and the Bulgarian Border Police opened our doors to gather our passports and take them away for processing. They were a serious and non-smiling bunch, staring several times between the photo and ourselves before believing we were who we said we were. Half an hour or so later, Iain's name was being called out and he was told that he had to accompany the even more serious-looking guards to the office. An hour later he was still not back.

Chapter 27
Dogs

Neither of us had ever been to Bulgaria before. Therefore, I reasoned, it was impossible that Iain could have done anything wrong in order to warrant being detained at passport control. However, I knew nothing about Bulgaria either, and therefore concluded that it must be highly corrupt and Iain was currently under arrest as he had been framed for a crime that he hadn't committed. The mind can play all sorts of tricks, especially when tired. Thankfully, after a further hour of brain rumination, Iain and his passport were returned to our compartment.

Apparently, Iain had spent his time in an office with several burly, unsmiling uniformed guards, all with guns. They had barked "sit" to Iain whilst pointing at a chair and then spent the entire hour and a half staring between the passport photo and him, whilst one of the others was also reading something on a computer screen. Only one of the guards spoke English and asked him if he had ever been to Austria, to which he truthfully replied "yes". They then continued to stare before eventually saying, "You are wanted by Austria, but you can go now." The whole thing was most bizarre and fairly intimidating. We were both relieved when the train pulled away again and puzzled as to what on earth Austria wanted Iain for.

Iain had been to Austria three times, once on this trip where, due to the Schengen agreement, they wouldn't even have known that we had passed through. Another time was to take our son to a ski academy which we combined with a family ski holiday, and finally once more when researching the setting up of a ski company. As far as he was aware, none of these things constituted a criminal act, and also as far as he was aware, during these times he had not committed any crimes.

We arrived in Sofia two hours late (thanks mainly to Iain), hungry, dirty and tired and were greeted by an "out of order" sign on the lift doors. We had to carry our bikes and luggage down two flights of stairs. Iain could manage his entire ensemble as one entity, almost carrying it on his back. I couldn't and I either had to unhitch everything and run up and down the stairs several times and then bump down the bike, or (and this was what happened more often) Iain very kindly came up and either helped me carry mine, or carried it for me (what a gentleman). Honestly, trains and hotels were often the same, more hassle than actually cycling and camping.

The traffic out of the city was so awful that we decided to take the next local train on to the next smaller town and to continue cycling from there. Before we could do that, however, we had to carry our bikes and all the equipment back up the bloody stairs.

We boarded yet another filthy train (although to be fair, it was not quite as dirty as the night train) and loaded all of our luggage onto two seats opposite us. As the train filled up, we had to move it all several times, as we seemed particularly talented at choosing the pre-allocated seats. We ended up sitting opposite a lady wearing a T-shirt with sparkly letters spelling out the word FUCK. Before she sat down, she placed a cardboard box very carefully on the luggage rack above her. When a tramp, or maybe just a scruffy, smelly old man, sat next to us, the FUCK T-shirt lady talked to him for a couple of minutes. She then stood up, got her precious box down from the luggage rack, carefully took out what looked like a large brown loaf stuffed with filling of some description, wrapped it in a plastic bag and placed it in his bag. We thought he asked her for the box too and she nodded calmly and carefully folded it flat and put it in his bag. Surely that had to be an example of THE most inappropriately labelled human being, ever!

They both departed and we were left alone in our compartment for a minute or two until we were joined by a young Hispanic-looking guy in jeans, clearly distressed and busy texting on his phone. Some minutes later, a transvestite (maybe transgender) person arrived and chose to stand in the corridor outside the compartment. He or she appeared to be a boy dressed as a girl, with heavily drawn-on girly eyebrows, full face make-up and wearing a girl's jacket. The transsexual talked to the Hispanic man for a few minutes and then was joined by another three from the LGBT (lesbian, gay, bisexual, transgender) community, who were all now gesticulating and seemed to be hurling abuse towards the Hispanic man. We weren't really expecting that. It was clear that they were all a tad angry and we were a bit concerned we might become inadvertently involved in some type of weird bitch-fight. It also seemed likely that the Hispanic man had come to seek refuge in the company of others (unrelated to the ongoing disagreement – whatever it was). We both decided to keep quiet. If either party realised we couldn't understand a word of what they were saying, our inadvertent peace-keeping role might just become a little less effective. We were extremely relieved that it didn't escalate, and even more so when the LGBT contingent left the train at the next station and the Hispanic man left the compartment. I hate acronyms and initialisms, but on this occasion, WTF!?

After our surreal train ride, we were rather pleased to be back on our bikes and back at the mercy of the surface, terrain and the weather. Our useless strip maps were now redundant, as we hadn't expected to be crossing Bulgaria, so we picked up a road map from a petrol garage. It wasn't great, as it was for cars and the scale was huge, but it wasn't really much worse than what we had become used to, and at least we now had an overview of the surrounding countryside too. It meant we could now deviate if we didn't like the road for some reason. Maybe we should have thought of it sooner! We were now really quite efficient at cycling and could speed up hills almost as if not carrying any weight, which was a blessing because it was hilly. More often than not, we would now be the overtaking cyclists. We were really enjoying ourselves on the bikes, feeling the benefits of being fitter, and on most days were covering about 100km with ease. Compared to the novices who set off from Roscoff, we were almost professionals. Whereas in the beginning I wasn't able to cycle through a shallow patch of gravel without falling off, I was now able to tackle (almost with finesse) deep mud or Brighton beach and remain upright and undertake slow manoeuvres without toppling ungracefully over sideways.

We were not quite so pleased to now be at the mercy of Bulgarian dogs. Most Bulgarians (well, in the area we passed through anyway, I have no way of confirming this as a bona fide fact) seem to be of the opinion that it is necessary to keep a dog, but unlike most Brit dogs, whose main purpose in life is to just be the family pet, Bulgarian dogs are given much more responsibility. They are there to guard and protect their property. If only the Bulgarian dogs actually knew the boundaries of their property and their jurisdiction. In the countryside we would cycle past a track or driveway to a farm or rural property and would hear the dog barking and running towards us. Nine times out of ten, the dog would also chase us along the road. Iain and I are confident around dogs, so mostly we weren't too bothered, and we could usually cycle faster than they could be bothered to run. Every now and again the dog would get a bit close for comfort, but mostly they were not too aggressive, and as long as we were heading away from their property they seemed to be happy that they had performed their doggy duties. We were lucky, however, and didn't come across the packs of wild dogs that we had heard reported from Romania. Our main gripe was the dogs' contribution to our complete lack of sleep. Every night we camped in Bulgaria we were kept awake more or less all night (even with earplugs) by barking and howling dogs. The bloody blighters were left outside all night and spent the entire time engrossed in some type of doggy bush telegraph system with each other. No wonder they couldn't be bothered to run fast.

Chapter 28
Third time unlucky

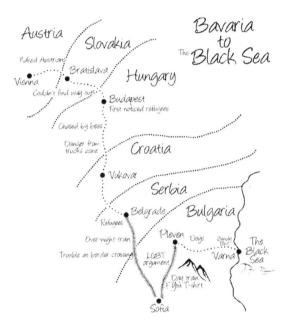

Austria

Slovakia

Bavaria
to
The Black Sea

Naked Austrians

Vienna

Bratislava

Couldn't find way out!

Hungary

Budapest
First noticed refugees

Chased by bees

Danger from
trucks zone

Croatia

Vukovar

Serbia

Belgrade

Bulgaria

Refugees

Over-night train

Pleven

Dogs

Bendy
Bus

Trouble at border crossing

LGBT
argument

Varna

The
Black
Sea

Day train
+ Ufo T-shirt

Sofia

We arrived in Varna (aka Bapho), a town on the shores of the Black Sea, at 9pm. Not really the best timing as we couldn't see the sea at all. We had the address of a campsite, but with the map not having enough detail on it, we could not pinpoint exactly where it was. Other than estimating it was probably a five-minute cycle along the coast, we had no idea. We asked at a taxi rank, and due to the late hour were happy to pay and follow him if it wasn't easy to find. The first driver we asked had never heard of it, but the second said it was about 12–14km away. Bugger!

Due to the late hour, we decided to book into a cheap hotel, order a pizza and pretend to arrive the next day!

It was a good call despite being on the second floor and having to endure the penultimate round of the transporting-the-luggage-up-the-stairs game. The pizza arrived with free cake, which was the best cake I had tasted since France and, due to dog-induced sleep deprivation, we both slept like logs for over nine hours.

We decided breakfast on THE beach at THE BLACK SEA was in order. With the final round of the transporting-the-luggage game completed, we loaded up our bikes for the final time and were pleased we had delayed our arrival at the final destination until daylight hours. It felt great to be on the bikes, knowing we had achieved SO much. We were also happy it was a Sunday, so hopefully the traffic wouldn't be so bad. How wrong could we have been.

Within seconds, the back end of a "bendy bus" clipped Iain and almost took him out. It was the closest that either of us had come to being wiped out. It was an awful thing for me to witness and even worse for Iain to experience. All just minutes from our final destination. How ironic, of all the things that we had encountered that perhaps would have sounded interesting or heroic on an obituary, "Bendy bus on the final roundabout" didn't have quite the same ring.

Thankfully, shortly after the bendy-bus incident we were able to take to the pavement and got our first sight of the Black Sea. It's not black, just in case you are wondering. It was a beautiful shade of aquamarine blue and was fringed by wonderfully fine light-golden sand. So thumbs up to the parts supplied by nature. Between the beach and the promenade were huge high walls, each belonging to a (mostly) tacky bar and blocking the view to the beach and sea. Thumbs down to man-made constructions. In need of breakfast, we chose a café spot which had a wooden walkway down to the sea, so that after we had eaten we could ride the bikes down to the waterside.

We've never had cheese on toast for breakfast before. It was disappointing and not quite the celebratory meal we had envisaged, but it was the best option. We then wheeled (due to cycling prohibited signs!) our bikes down the boardwalk, took some photos, and almost went for a swim, but it was too cold, so we opted for a paddle instead. It was really weird. We had actually made it, cycled almost 5,000km, but it seemed like a big anti-climax. There was no party. The challenge had suddenly, in that act of arrival, just finished, fizzled out, gone. In that moment it didn't seem like a big achievement, more just like a lot of separate disjointed experiences, some a lot more memorable than others, some becoming a bit kind of bland in their similarity (tent down, pack up, ride, shop, unpack, eat, tent up, sleep), with not much to differentiate one day from another. The overriding emotion was not the joy we had expected but a sense of grief. It was over. We didn't want it to be over; we had experienced the most incredible times, and the simplicity of just getting on a bike and pedalling into the unknown each day was something we didn't want to lose.

Both quiet and contemplative, we ordered another drink and then headed off to find the campsite. The first 3km or so were quite pleasant and along the promenade. A sulphur smell in our noses brought to our attention that we were passing a rustic-looking thermal bath. Natural hot water had both been diverted into a random collection of shower heads which were fixed haphazardly along a crumbling wall and was being collected in rusty buckets. Elderly gentlemen sat with their feet in the buckets playing chess on the beach, whilst the ladies sat and chatted.

When the promenade came to an end we had a steep hairpin hill to ride up. It was hard work, but achievable, and I think we were both relishing, once again, our newly developed ability. At the top we confirmed with the lady selling Manchester United towels that we were heading towards the main highway. It was a particularly hot and humid day, and as I finished my water at the top of the hill, I didn't worry as we only had about 8km left to cycle. We should arrive within half an hour.

The bad news was that the main highway was a fast-moving dual carriageway. Being Sunday and a beach resort, it was also particularly busy. We decided it was safer to stick to the rough path at the side of the road. We had made it this far and almost felt like we would be tempting fate by cycling on this of all roads on our last day. The path soon deteriorated into a rocky, broken brick and sandy mess with obstacles like trees, dustbins, rubbish, parked cars and barbed wire thrown in for good measure. Progress was slow, very slow.

We couldn't find Street 20, the street that we were looking for. There were no signs and we couldn't find any people who knew what street they were in. For old times' sake, of course, every road that we investigated meant cycling up yet another unnecessary hill. We crossed over the fast, noisy and dangerous dual carriageway several times but with no luck. Eventually, we came across a man fixing a motorbike, who informed us that it was about 6km back the way we had just come from, on the other side of the road. I'm a bit ashamed to admit it, but I had a bit of a melt-down! About three hours ago I had drunk the last of my water and had been expecting to arrive at the campsite within half an hour. I cried, shouted and cursed at the bloody shitty road, crappy pavement and fucking Lebara mobile company, because if they hadn't been SO incompetent we could have rung the campsite owner for directions and saved ourselves over two hours of horrendously hot hassle. We then pushed our bikes for 6km, because the "pavement" had deteriorated so much and was now also extremely narrow. We passed a large sign which informed us the road was a "Danger Zone!" (no shit, Sherlock).

Thankfully, the bike mechanic was right, wasn't winding us up like the aforementioned Hungarian campsite hoaxer, and after a 6km walk, we arrived at the right street. Onward and upward we pedalled, now searching for number 67. As the road levelled out we cycled past a small shop and then a series of larger properties. Just like in the countryside, each had a resident dog. The road split into three options, and as we were busy looking for house numbers, two vicious-looking dogs (one German Shepherd and one Heinz 57) were snarling, foaming at the mouth and barking angrily at us. "Glad they're behind bars," I said to Iain at just the exact same moment that the German Shepherd somehow squeezed himself between the bars and free. "Shit," we both said and cycled off as fast as we possibly could. Several minutes later, surprised that a dog of that size hadn't caught up with me, I nervously took a look round and for the first time realised, with great relief, that it only had three legs. Phew! We then discovered that we had chosen the wrong option where the road split, and we would have to go back past the dogs. We decided to walk this time, and they didn't even bark.

We found the campsite, which actually was just someone's front lawn. From the front lawn owner we received a warm welcome and a delicious cup of tea and found out he was an expat called Mike, looking to move on soon to Tenerife once he had sold his house and aforementioned lawn.

We spent the evening, after the usual camping rigmarole, discussing what we should do with the rest of our six months off now that we had finished our challenge. We planned to spend time off the bikes, with our son in France, then some time with friends, and then to spend our final three weeks cycling home to our daughter in Devon from Bordeaux along the EV1 route which runs up the west coast of France. This would more than make up for the small bit of train journey that we had opted for.

Mike's garden had magnificent internet coverage and the following day we booked flights and made arrangements for our final plans. Our bikes would need to be taken to pieces and put into boxes or bike bags for their journey. We would also need to buy larger bags in which to place all of our pannier bags. As luck would have it, Mike's partner's colleague Alex was also planning to fly with a bike and he knew where we could get bike boxes. After a hot and crowded bus ride into Varna town, we rendezvoused with Alex by the cathedral and he walked us to a bike shop – we would have never found it on our own. We were kindly supplied with free boxes and told which shop to buy duct tape and bags from.

We had a coffee with Alex (also a Brit), who told us he had spent several years teaching English after he had taken a Russian degree. He had married a woman from the Ukraine but had now had enough of Eastern Europe. He thought bigger trouble was brewing and was keen to get back to the UK for a peaceful life. He relayed some of his frustrations of living in Bulgaria, which were mainly summarised as no rules and no decent healthcare. A doctor had told him he could do surgery for him for a good price. A second opinion suggested he didn't actually need surgery. There had recently been protests and strikes in Bulgaria demanding a stop to corruption, but he thought it had not made any difference.

We headed back to Mike's garden in a taxi with our boxes, new bags and several rolls of tape. Mike offered to give us a lift to the airport for our flight booked in a couple of days. Ironically, in order to get to Nice, France, we had to fly via Stanstead, UK. We spent the rest of the day organising our kit and repacking it ready for the flight and found out that Mike and his partner were also leaving Bulgaria. He had spent eleven years there but hadn't found it the most friendly place to be. After a brief spell back in the UK, they were planning to move to the Canary Islands.

The following morning was spent taking the bikes to pieces so that they fitted into the boxes and taping them up so they were secure for the flight. We felt sad seeing them in that state, and apart from my bike being just a tad too big (for which the bike itself cannot be blamed), they had served us incredibly well. We'd had no mechanical issues and hadn't even had one puncture between us. We hoped they would survive their boxed-up flight without incident or injury. Good old Solo and Polo.

After a day relaxing on the beach, we headed for the airport, wished Mike all the best, and deposited Solo, Polo and our bags at the "outsized luggage" check-in. We headed through security with our hand luggage and then queued for passport control. I was waved through by a short, round, moustachioed lady with a gun. I was thinking "I'm sure I met a relative of yours in the train ticket office in Budapest." Iain was told to wait by the same lady. "Oh no," I thought, "Here we go again."

Several minutes later, Iain was still waiting. I was told to move around the corner by Ms Moustache. I was not going to argue: she had a gun and a moustache! Eventually, a serious-looking uniformed officer arrived. He didn't smile. He just said, "This way" to Iain and then added, "The Austrians want to speak to you."

Epilogue

Once again, Iain managed to escape the clutches of the Austrian authorities. The Bulgarians released him just before our flight left, mainly (we think) because the Austrians couldn't be bothered to answer their phone calls. Or maybe it was just his lucky day, again. We are still none the wiser as to why the Austrians want to speak to him. They have our details. Maybe one day they will let us know.

We raised just over £9,000 for our chosen charity, CHICKS, one we still have close links with and support wholeheartedly. A big thanks to everyone who supported us by donating to them. To appease any sense of guilt – due to the miles covered by train – we completed our trip with a few hundred miles of extra cycling up the west coast of France, from Bordeaux to Roscoff. On this return journey, we noticed that someone had kindly ironed out all of the hills. Particularly those encountered in the early chapters!

On arrival at the Black Sea, we had both felt bereft in that moment when the act of reaching the goal swiftly extinguished the challenge. At that time, there wasn't any sense of the whole journey adding up to one big achievement, more like just a lot of separate disjointed experiences. Retrospectively, in some ways it still seems a bit like that. However, the rose-tinted spectacles of passing time have finally worked their magic. The feeling that "we actually made it", that we had cycled (almost) 5,000km, that we two (almost) normal (almost) old people who were complete novice cyclists had actually powered themselves by pedal across the whole of Europe, has finally reached us and it's something that we are now pretty proud of.

We are not expert adventurers. We can't be – I'm still beardless and we didn't resort to eating just bread and jam! However, it's fair to say that we are now hooked on the freedom, simplicity and adventure that just getting on a bike and pedalling into the unknown every day brings. It's a way of life that we would dearly love to repeat. Unsurprisingly to all who know us, we are currently planning an even bigger challenge for the not-too-distant future. We would love to hear from you if our challenge has in any way inspired you to have your own adventure, no matter how big or small.

If you'd like to see just how big my bike was, leave your details on my Beardless Adventurer website and I'll send you a photo. I'll also let you know when my next book is out. You have my word, I will send you nothing else!

Thank you so much for reading my book; I hope you enjoyed it. I'd be most appreciative if you'd leave me an Amazon review. It really is the best and most authentic way to spread the word to other book lovers, backed up, of course, by a bit of old-fashioned word of mouth.

About the author

Prior to writing this book, Donna admits to dabbling in at least twenty different jobs, with a variety of interest levels! She relishes in the unexpected experiences associated with new places and people. Her insatiable appetite for learning has found her studying subjects as diverse as Ancient Eastern Medicine, Science, English language, Midwifery, Nordic walking and Bush-craft. She describes herself as a bit of a knowledge junkie.

Since leaving emergency ambulance work, Donna has possessed an unbounded desire to live life to the full, as she says you can't plan when your time is up. She and her husband currently live on Dartmoor National Park, in the UK, running an outdoor activity centre for children, amongst other things!

If interested, you can follow and say hi to Donna – The Beardless Adventurer on the following social media channels:

www.facebook.com/beardlessadventurer

www.twitter.com/@DonnaAshton

A final word from Donna

It's a lonely old game being an author and I'd love to hear from you. Whether it's tales from your own adventures, no matter how big or small, feedback about this book or what inspired you, whatever your age, to attempt something out of the ordinary. Please do send a message to me: donna@beardlessadventurer.com

www.beardlessadventurer.com

Appendix:
Bikes and kit

Bikes

Solo – Iain's bike
Koga Traveller
Male frame, size 57
Frame size: Over-sized tubes made from triple hardened aluminium 7005
Weight: 16kg
Gears: 30
Shimano Diore LX components
Brakes: Magura hydraulic rim brakes
Wheels: Koga Q-guard, quick release with integrated derailleur protector (this is what the bike shop got excited about – and I did too, eventually!)
Specialist tyres – Vredestein Perfect Tour Sportex 40-622, allegedly puncture proof and with double eyelet rims
Integrated rear carrier structure: i.e. pannier rack
Lights: front and rear powered by an integral hub dynamo.
Integral rear wheel bike stand.

Bike constructed (according to its own cute passport/owner's manual) by William.

Polo – Donna's bike
Koga Traveller, the same as Iain's, except for the following:
Female frame, size 47

Weight 16.3kg (note, heavier than Iain's bike)
Constructed by Eithan.

We attached our own front luggage racks.

We have nothing but praise for these bikes. They were reliable, performed better than we did and required no actual repairs for the entire trip. We did, however, look after them well with regular cleaning and oiling. Although we didn't believe the tyres would actually be puncture-proof (and sensibly carried spare inner tubes), they proved us wrong and not once did we get a flat or need to get out a patch or the repair kit.

Panniers and bags
We used waterproof bags from a company called CARRADICE.
The models we used were the Carradry. They had quick-clip pannier hooks (for up to 13mm racks).

Front bags
Capacity 10 litres each (27cm wide × 35cm high × 11cm depth), no pockets.

Rear bags

Capacity 29 litres each (32cm wide × 51cm high × 16cm depth), with a rear zip pocket compartment and a small internal zip pocket (for valuables etc.).

These were substantially less in cost (approx half the price) than Ortlieb's, and, apart from the zip pocket on the rear bag (currently being redesigned by the company), were completely waterproof, and both the bags and clip mechanisms performed excellently.

Handlebar bags

Donna – Ortlieb (compact 6)

Iain –Altura Orkney (7 litre – waterproof) available in most bike shops or online.

We each then had a dry bag on top of our rear panniers which held our sleep mats. Iain's also held the tent, while mine held my chair.

How we carried stuff

Iain carried the tent, I carried the bedding.

Iain carried the cooking equipment (stove, pans, washing-up liquid), I carried the plates, cutlery, and food.

We each carried our own clothing.

My front left (traffic side) pannier was dedicated to things that might be or might get wet. So, waterproof clothing, wash kit, travel towel, sarong, bikini, washing line, washing powder, unwashed clothes.

My front right (drier side on the continent) was where my entire travelling wardrobe lived!

The rear right was where the bedding lived, on top of contact lenses, glasses, medication and a spare notebook with the internal pocket used for important documents, phone chargers and the iPod.

In a separate dry bag, for convenience kept in the top of the bag, I kept a set of merino wool clothing, hat, head-torch and a change of clothes for after a day's cycling (a kind of grab bag to head straight into the shower or tent with).

The external pocket was used for a comprehensive first aid kit. This bag was always full.

The rear left was our kitchen store cupboard. The weight of this bag varied enormously depending on how much food we were carrying. (The grab bag above could be transferred to this one when light.)

I have no idea how Iain arranged his bags, he can't remember, but it obviously worked for him!

Tent

Can't really recommend the first one.
The second one, which was great, was from Decathlon.
Quechua Quick Hiker
3-man
Weight: 3.3kg

Bedding

Mats: ThermaRest Basecamp (5cm thick, navy)
Donna's – medium
Iain's – Alpkit Dirtbag XL (it's thicker than 5cm at head and tapers to thinner at foot end)
Double feather duvet (summer weight)
Double fitted sheet, later replaced by 2 × Alpkit Cloud Cover (goose down) as much more compact (520g)
Plus Iain now also sleeps on a sheepskin.

Cooking paraphernalia

2 × Trangia stoves, which run on methylated spirits (or similar).
Although these types of fuel stoves burn slowly (so cooking can take a while), we were uncertain what type of gas cylinders would be available the further east we travelled, and so thought a meths stove (which can and did try all sorts of funny-coloured liquid) would be more versatile. The meths-type fuel was always cheap too. We were happy with our choice.

1 litre bottle of methylated spirits (a lighter)
2 × stands for pans
1 × lightweight aluminium folding windbreak (essential)
Russian doll-type set of lightweight saucepans: 2 pans with fold-out handles, 1 frying pan (separate handle)
1 tiny kettle
2 wooden spoons

Several small plastic bottles containing salt, pepper, oil, herbs, spices, vinegar

1 tiny plastic chopping board.

1 tiny bottle of washing-up liquid

1 sponge scourer

1 tea towel.

We each had:

Set of cutlery (lightweight titanium)

Small spoon – thank you, Jon Mac, spoon carver extraordinaire

Folding-handled, metal camping cup (rubbish) – We threw these away, as the cups stayed hot despite the liquid in the cup becoming cold – burnt lips cold drink!

Plastic glass (perfect) – We used these after throwing cups away for both hot drinks and (more importantly) wine.

Plastic plate – I didn't like them, but they lasted, were light, and did the job

Small plastic bowl with lid – Served well as both bowls and extra food storage containers

Opinel knife

LOTS of zip-lock bags (both medium and large sizes)

Iain also carried a plastic coffee mug with integral cafetière plunger.

One small very cheap cool-bag (single packed-lunch size). We had no cool packs, but by packing all of the cold stuff together it did stay cool for the whole day, so worthwhile.

Clothing

This is just to give you an idea of how much clothing I took. Iain can't remember what he packed!

2 × cycling-type T-shirts (lightweight coconut fibre)

2 × cycling shorts (one gel, one foam)

2 × cycling skirts (to wear over shorts as I don't like the Lycra-clad look)

2 × fleeces (one for cycling in, one for other)

1 × merino wool leggings (for night and under-layer if particularly cold evening)

1 × merino wool long-sleeve top (for night and under-layer if particularly cold evening)

1 × pair fluffy socks

1 × shirt and 1 × skirt (for non-cycling days)

1 × trousers (lightweight hiking type)

1 × thin down jacket (from Decathlon) (also doubled as extra pillow filling)

1 × waterproof jacket

1 × waterproof trousers (but didn't like them – mostly it seemed better just to get wet legs)

1 × sunhat (peaked baseball cap type – used when cycling)

1 × bikini and 1 × sarong

2 sets of underwear (for when not cycling)

2 × sports bra (for when cycling)

1 × pair of Teva sandal/shoe for cycling (Donna)

1 × pair of flip-flops (aka thongs) for off the bike

Iain cycled in lightweight Merrill trainers and off-bike had other shoes. Plus Crocs for in the shower.

Cycle shorts

These really do seem to be a matter of whatever you are most comfortable with. There does not seem to be one type of amazing cycle short which suits everyone out there.

In my experience, I would say buy the best quality (preferably gel) ones you can afford. The protection that they offer hugely outweighed the unpleasant but not painful walking in a nappy feeling. However, make sure you get the size right – if they are even a touch too small the lack of circulation in your legs will become painful.

Conversely, Iain started with gel cycle shorts. Again, he found the legs too tight and restrictive, so then he tried some other foam-type ones, but also found the leg restriction so annoying that he completed most of the trip without either.

Safety equipment and tools etc.

We both chose to wear cycling helmets on busy or main roads (but not off-road or on cycle paths).

We thought it sensible to decorate our bikes with reflective jackets for some sections.

Our bikes have integral dynamo lights (which meant we could leave them on whenever on road)

We took oil, an old toothbrush and a small cloth to maintain the chains about once a week.

We took a spare inner tube each and a puncture repair kit/ tyre levers.

We both had a head torch.
Insurance (medical AND for the bikes and equipment)
1 × first aid kit (any personal medication)
Sun screen

Random

2 × Helinox Chair-One
1 × travel washing line (twisted elastic means you don't need pegs)
Small fold-up bowl (we used this only when wild camping)
2 × notebooks and pen (Donna)
2 × passports

Electronic gadgets

1 × basic phone + charger
1 × small tablet
1 × Kindle ebook reader
1 × camera
1 × battery pack – suitable for charging everything

Interestingly, if we went for longer, we would probably still need and take the same amount of stuff. If we went on a shorter trip there's a few things we could leave behind like the washing line and Kindle, but essentially this would be our packing list.